Acidaminococcaceae: Gut
Acidaminococcaceae: Genital
Acidobacteriaceae: Nose
Actinomycetaceae: Gut
Actinomycetaceae: Nose
Actinomycetaceae: Mouth
Actinomycetaceae: Genital
Actinomycetaceae: Ear
Aerococcaceae: Gut
Aerococcaceae: Nose
Aerococcaceae: Mouth
Aeromonadaceae: Genital
Alcaligenaceae: Gut
Alcaligenaceae: Nose
Alcaligenaceae: Genital
Alicyclobacillaceae: Gut
Anaeroplasmataceae: Genital
Bacillaceae: Gut
Bacillaceae: Nose
Bacillaceae: Mouth
Bacillaceae: Genital
Bacillaceae: Hand
Bacteroidaceae: Gut
Bacteroidaceae: Nose
Bacteroidaceae: Mouth
Bacteroidaceae: Genital
Bacteroidaceae: Ear
Bacteroidaceae: Hand
Bartonellaceae: Nose
Bifidobacteriaceae: Gut
Bifidobacteriaceae: Nose
Bifidobacteriaceae: Mouth
Bifidobacteriaceae: Genital
Bifidobacteriaceae: Ear
Bifidobacteriaceae: Hand
Brevibacteriaceae: Gut
Brevibacteriaceae: Mouth
Burkholderiaceae: Gut
Burkholderiaceae: Nose
Burkholderiaceae: Mouth
Burkholderiaceae: Genital
Caldicoprobacteraceae: Gut
Campylobacteraceae: Gut
Campylobacteraceae: Nose
Campylobacteraceae: Genital
Cardiobacteriaceae: Nose
Carnobacteriaceae: Gut
Carnobacteriaceae: Nose
Carnobacteriaceae: Genital
Caulobacteraceae: Gut
Caulobacteraceae: Hand
Christensenellaceae: Gut
Clostridiaceae: Gut
Clostridiaceae: Nose
Clostridiaceae: Genital
Clostridiaceae: Ear
Clostridiaceae: Hand
Clostridiales Family XI.
 Incertae Sedis: Gut
Clostridiales Family XI.
 Incertae Sedis: Nose
Clostridiales Family XI.
 Incertae Sedis: Mouth
Clostridiales Family XI.
 Incertae Sedis: Genital
Clostridiales Family XI.
 Incertae Sedis: Ear

Clostridiales Family XIII.
 Incertae Sedis: Gut
Clostridiales Family XIII.
 Incertae Sedis: Nose
Clostridiales Family XIII.
 Incertae Sedis: Ear
Comamonadaceae: Gut
Comamonadaceae: Nose
Comamonadaceae: Genital
Coriobacteriaceae: Gut
Coriobacteriaceae: Nose
Coriobacteriaceae: Genital
Coriobacteriaceae: Ear
Coriobacteriaceae: Hand
Corynebacteriaceae: Gut
Corynebacteriaceae: Nose
Corynebacteriaceae: Mouth
Corynebacteriaceae: Genital
Corynebacteriaceae: Hand
Cytophagaceae: Nose
Cytophagaceae: Genital
Desulfovibrionaceae: Gut
Desulfovibrionaceae: Nose
Desulfovibrionaceae: Genital
Desulfovibrionaceae: Mouth
Desulfovibrionaceae: Hand
Enterobacteriaceae: Gut
Enterobacteriaceae: Genital
Enterobacteriaceae: Ear
Enterobacteriaceae: Hand
Enterococcaceae: Gut
Enterococcaceae: Nose
Erysipelotrichaceae: Gut
Erysipelotrichaceae: Nose
Erysipelotrichaceae: Genital
Erysipelotrichaceae: Ear
Erysipelotrichaceae: Hand
Eubacteriaceae: Gut
Fibrobacteraceae: Gut
Fibrobacteraceae: Ear
Flavobacteriaceae: Gut
Flavobacteriaceae: Nose
Flavobacteriaceae: Genital
Flavobacteriaceae: Ear
Fusobacteriaceae: Nose
Fusobacteriaceae: Genital
Geodermatophilaceae: Nose
Geodermatophilaceae: Genital
Hydrogenophilaceae: Genital
Hyphomicrobiaceae: Nose
Intrasporangiaceae: Nose
Intrasporangiaceae: Mouth
Kineosporiaceae: Nose
Kofleriaceae: Gut
Lachnospiraceae: Gut
Lachnospiraceae: Nose
Lachnospiraceae: Mouth
Lachnospiraceae: Genital
Lachnospiraceae: Ear
Lachnospiraceae: Hand
Lactobacillaceae: Gut
Lactobacillaceae: Nose
Lactobacillaceae: Mouth
Lactobacillaceae: Genital
Lactobacillaceae: Ear
Legionellaceae: Gut
Leptotrichiaceae: Nose

Leptotrichiaceae: Mouth
Leptotrichiaceae: Genital
Leuconostocaceae: Mouth
Methanobacteriaceae: Genital
Methylobacteriaceae: Gut
Methylobacteriaceae: Genital
Methylophilaceae: Genital
Microbacteriaceae: Gut
Microbacteriaceae: Mouth
Micrococcaceae: Gut
Micrococcaceae: Nose
Micrococcaceae: Mouth
Micrococcaceae: Genital
Mogibacteriaceae: Gut
Mogibacteriaceae: Hand
Moraxellaceae: Nose
Moraxellaceae: Mouth
Moraxellaceae: Genital
Mycobacteriaceae: Gut
Mycobacteriaceae: Nose
Mycobacteriaceae: Mouth
Neisseriaceae: Nose
Neisseriaceae: Genital
Nocardioidaceae: Gut
Nocardioidaceae: Genital
Odoribacteraceae: Gut
Odoribacteraceae: Hand
Oscillospiraceae: Gut
Oscillospiraceae: Nose
Oscillospiraceae: Ear
Oxalobacteraceae: Gut
Oxalobacteraceae: Nose
Oxalobacteraceae: Genital
Oxalobacteraceae: Hand
Pasteurellaceae: Gut
Pasteurellaceae: Nose
Pasteurellaceae: Mouth
Pasteurellaceae: Genital
Pasteurellaceae: Ear
Peptococcaceae: Gut
Peptococcaceae: Nose
Peptococcaceae: Ear
Peptostreptococcaceae: Gut
Peptostreptococcaceae: Nose
Peptostreptococcaceae:
 Mouth
Peptostreptococcaceae:
 Genital
Peptostreptococcaceae: Ear
Peptostreptococcaceae: Hand
Planctomycetaceae: Mouth
Planococcaceae: Mouth
Porphyromonadaceae: Gut
Porphyromonadaceae: Nose
Porphyromonadaceae: Mouth
Porphyromonadaceae: Genital
Porphyromonadaceae: Ear
Porphyromonadaceae: Hand
Prevotellaceae: Gut
Prevotellaceae: Nose
Prevotellaceae: Mouth
Prevotellaceae: Genital
Prevotellaceae: Ear
Prevotellaceae: Hand
Propionibacteriaceae: Gut
Propionibacteriaceae: Nose
Propionibacteriaceae: Mouth

Propionibacteriaceae: Genital
Propionibacteriaceae: Nose
Rhizobiaceae: Mouth
Rhizobiaceae: Genital
Rhizobiaceae: Nose
Rhizobiaceae: Genital
Rhodobacteraceae: Nose
Rhodobacteraceae: Mouth
Rhodospirillaceae: Gut
Rhodospirillaceae: Nose
Rhodospirillaceae: Genital
Rikenellaceae: Gut
Rikenellaceae: Nose
Rikenellaceae: Genital
Rikenellaceae: Ear
Rikenellaceae: Hand
Ruminococcaceae: Gut
Ruminococcaceae: Nose
Ruminococcaceae: Mouth
Ruminococcaceae: Genital
Ruminococcaceae: Ear
Ruminococcaceae: Hand
Solanaceae: Nose
Solirubrobacteraceae: Gut
Sphingobacteriaceae: Gut
Sphingomonadaceae: Nose
Sphingomonadaceae: Mouth
Sphingomonadaceae: Genital
Staphylococcaceae: Gut
Staphylococcaceae: Nose
Staphylococcaceae: Mouth
Staphylococcaceae: Genital
Staphylococcaceae: Hand
Streptococcaceae: Gut
Streptococcaceae: Nose
Streptococcaceae: Mouth
Streptococcaceae: Genital
Streptococcaceae: Ear
Streptococcaceae: Hand
Sutterellaceae: Gut
Sutterellaceae: Nose
Sutterellaceae: Genital
Sutterellaceae: Ear
Synergistaceae: Gut
Synergistaceae: Nose
Thermaceae: Gut
Thermaceae: Nose
Thermaceae: Genital
Tissierellaceae: Gut
Tissierellaceae: Hand
Trueperaceae: Nose
Veillonellaceae: Gut
Veillonellaceae: Nose
Veillonellaceae: Mouth
Veillonellaceae: Genital
Veillonellaceae: Ear
Veillonellaceae: Hand
Verrucomicrobiaceae: Gut
Verrucomicrobiaceae: Nose
Verrucomicrobiaceae: Ear
Verrucomicrobiaceae: Hand
Victivallaceae: Gut
Xanthomonadaceae: Gut
Xanthomonadaceae: Mouth
Xanthomonadaceae:
 Genital

| | | | | |
|---|---|---|---|---|
| Bisphenol A | Lead | 4-Hydroxyphenanthrene | PCB-178 | PCB-7 |
| PBB-153 | Lithium | 6-Hydroxychrysene | PCB-179 | PCB-72 |
| PBB-28 | Manganese | 9-Hydroxyfluorene | PCB-18 + 30 | PCB-73 |
| BDE-10 | Mercury | 9-Hydroxyphenanthrene | PCB-180 + 193 | PCB-77 |
| BDE-100 | Molybdenum | Benzyl Paraben | PCB-181 | PCB-78 |
| BDE-105 | Nickel | Butyl Paraben | PCB-182 | PCB-79 |
| BDE-116 | Selenium | Ethyl Paraben | PCB-183 + 185 | PCB-8 |
| BDE-119 + 120 | Silver | Isopropyl Paraben | PCB-184 | PCB-80 |
| BDE-12 + 13 | Tellurium | Methyl Paraben | PCB-186 | PCB-81 |
| BDE-126 | Thallium | n-Propyl Paraben | PCB-187 | PCB-82 |
| BDE-128 | Thorium | Decachloro Biphenyl | PCB-188 | PCB-83 + 99 |
| BDE-138 + 166 | Tin | PCB-1 | PCB-189 | PCB-84 |
| BDE-140 | Total Arsenic | PCB-10 | PCB-19 | PCB-85 + 116 + 117 |
| BDE-15 | Tungsten | PCB-103 | PCB-190 | PCB-86 + 87 + 97 + 108 |
| BDE-153 | Uranium | PCB-104 | PCB-191 | + 119 + 125 |
| BDE-154 | Vanadium | PCB-105 | PCB-192 | PCB-88 + 91 |
| BDE-155 | Zinc | PCB-106 | PCB-194 | PCB-89 |
| BDE-17 + 25 | Aldrin | PCB-107 + 124 | PCB-195 | PCB-9 |
| BDE-181 | alpha-chlordane | PCB-109 | PCB-196 | PCB-90 + 101 + 113 |
| BDE-183 | cis-nonachlor | PCB-11 | PCB-197 + 200 | PCB-92 |
| BDE-190 | gamma-chlordane | PCB-110 + 115 | PCB-198 + 199 | PCB-93 + 95 + 98 + 100 |
| BDE-203 | gamma-HCH | PCB-111 | PCB-2 | + 102 |
| BDE-206 | Hexachlorobenzene | PCB-112 | PCB-20 + 28 | PCB-94 |
| BDE-207 | Mirex | PCB-114 | PCB-201 | PCB-96 |
| BDE-208 | Oxychlordane | PCB-118 | PCB-202 | PCB, Aroclor 1260 |
| BDE-209 | p,p'-DDE | PCB-12 + 13 | PCB-203 | PCB-101 |
| BDE-28 + 33 | p,p'-DDT | PCB-120 | PCB-204 | PCB-138 |
| BDE-30 | Plama B-HCH | PCB-121 | PCB-205 | PCB-28 |
| BDE-32 | Toxaphene, Parlar No. 26 | PCB-122 | PCB-206 | PCB-74 |
| BDE-35 | Toxaphene, Parlar No. 50 | PCB-123 | PCB-207 | PCB-99 |
| BDE-37 | trans-Nonachlor | PCB-126 | PCB-208 | PFBA |
| BDE-47 | 2,4'-DDD | PCB-127 | PCB-209 | PFBS |
| BDE-49 | 2,4'-DDE | PCB-128 + 166 | PCB-21 + 33 | PFDA |
| BDE-51 | 2,4'-DDT | PCB-129 + 138 + 160 + 163 | PCB-22 | PFDoA |
| BDE-66 | 4,4'-DDD | PCB-130 | PCB-23 | PFHpA |
| BDE-7 | 4,4'-DDE | PCB-131 | PCB-24 | PFHxA |
| BDE-71 | 4,4'-DDT | PCB-132 | PCB-25 | PFHxS |
| BDE-75 | Aldrin | PCB-133 | PCB-26 + 29 | PFNA |
| BDE-77 | alpha-Endosulphan | PCB-134 + 143 | PCB-27 | PFOA |
| BDE-79 | beta-Endosulphan | PCB-135 + 151 + 154 | PCB-3 | PFOS |
| BDE-8 + 11 | Chlordane, alpha (cis) | PCB-136 | PCB-31 | PFOSA |
| BDE-85 | Chlordane, gamma (trans) | PCB-137 | PCB-32 | PFPeA |
| BDE-99 | Chlordane, oxy- | PCB-139 + 140 | PCB-34 | PFUnA |
| 1,2,3,4,6,7,8-HPCDD | Dieldrin | PCB-14 | PCB-35 | 2-Isopropoxyphenol |
| 1,2,3,4,6,7,8-HPCDF | Endosulphan Sulphate | PCB-141 | PCB-36 | (propoxur) |
| 1,2,3,4,7,8-HXCDD | Endrin | PCB-142 | PCB-37 | 2,4-D |
| 1,2,3,4,7,8-HXCDF | Endrin Aldehyde | PCB-144 | PCB-38 | 2,4-Dichlorophenol |
| 1,2,3,4,7,8,9-HPCDF | Endrin Ketone | PCB-145 | PCB-39 | 2,4,5-Trichlorophenol |
| 1,2,3,6,7,8-HXCDD | HCH, alpha | PCB-146 | PCB-4 | 2,4,6-Trichlorophenol |
| 1,2,3,6,7,8-HXCDF | HCH, beta | PCB-147 + 149 | PCB-40 + 41 + 71 | 2,5-Dichlorophenol |
| 1,2,3,7,8-PECDD | HCH, delta | PCB-148 | PCB-42 | 3-PBA |
| 1,2,3,7,8-PECDF | HCH, gamma | PCB-15 | PCB-43 | 4-F-3-PBA |
| 1,2,3,7,8,9-HXCDD | Heptachlor | PCB-150 | PCB-44 + 47 + 65 | Carbofuranphenol |
| 1,2,3,7,8,9-HXCDF | Heptachlor Epoxide | PCB-152 | PCB-45 + 51 | cis-DBCA |
| 2,3,4,6,7,8-HXCDF | Methoxychlor | PCB-153 + 168 | PCB-46 | cis-DCCA |
| 2,3,4,7,8-PECDF | Nonachlor, cis- | PCB-155 | PCB-48 | Diethyldithiophosphate |
| 2,3,7,8-TCDD | Nonachlor, trans- | PCB-156 + 157 | PCB-49 + 69 | Diethylphosphate |
| 2,3,7,8-TCDF | 1-Hydroxybenz(a)anth- | PCB-158 | PCB-5 | Diethylthiophosphate |
| OCDD | racene | PCB-159 | PCB-50 + 53 | Dimethyldithiophosphate |
| OCDF | 1-Hydroxyphenanthrene | PCB-16 | PCB-52 | Dimethylphosphate |
| alpha-HBCDD | 1-Hydroxypyrene | PCB-161 | PCB-54 | Dimethylthiophosphate |
| beta-HBCDD | 1-Naphthol | PCB-162 | PCB-55 | Pentachlorophenol |
| gamma-HBCDD | 2-Hydroxychrysene | PCB-164 | PCB-56 | Trans-DCCA |
| Aluminium | 2-Hydroxyfluorene | PCB-165 | PCB-57 | MBP (n+iso) |
| Antimony | 2-Hydroxyphenanthrene | PCB-167 | PCB-58 | MBzP |
| Barium | 2-Naphthol | PCB-169 | PCB-59 + 62 + 75 | MCHP |
| Beryllium | 3-Hydroxybenz(a)anth- | PCB-17 | PCB-6 | MCPP |
| Bismuth | racene | PCB-170 | PCB-60 | MEHHP |
| Cadmium | 3-Hydroxybenzo(a)py-rene | PCB-171 + 173 | PCB-61 + 70 + 74 + 76 | MEHP |
| Cesium | 3-Hydroxychrysene | PCB-172 | PCB-63 | MEOHP |
| Chromium | 3-Hydroxyfluoranthene | PCB-174 | PCB-64 | MEP |
| Cobalt | 3-Hydroxyfluorene | PCB-175 | PCB-66 | MiNP |
| Copper | 3-Hydroxyphenanthrene | PCB-176 | PCB-67 | MMP |
| Iodine | 4-Hydroxychrysene | PCB-177 | PCB-68 | Triclosan |

# ANATOMIC
## ADAM DICKINSON

Coach House Books | Toronto

Published with the generous assistance of the Canada Council for the Arts and the Ontario Arts Council. Coach House Books also acknowledges the support of the Government of Canada through the Canada Book Fund and the Government of Ontario through the Ontario Book Publishing Tax Credit.

LIBRARY AND ARCHIVES CANADA CATALOGUING IN PUBLICATION

Dickinson, Adam, 1974-, author
　　Anatomic / Adam Dickinson.

Poems.
Issued in print and electronic formats.
ISBN 978-1-55245-364-3 (softcover).

　　I. Title.

PS8557.I3235A53 2018　　　　C811ʹ.6　　　　C2018-900929-2

Anatomic is available as an ebook: ISBN 978 1 77056 546 3 (EPUB), ISBN 978 1 77056 550 0 (PDF)

*For Ruby, Millicent, and Marigold,*
*with every μg*
*of my being*

The keys touch me when I type. My breath smells because other creatures live out their ends in my mouth. Wearing a waterproof jacket perverts my immune response. My throat is sore because of a miniature life form that, when magnified, looks like a string of pearls. My neighbour's attempt to control dandelions leads to misspellings in my adrenal gland. In my lower intestine, *E. coli* reproduces, making vitamin K and assisting with undigested carbohydrates. My fat collects signatures from one of the most profitable companies in the world. In necessary ways and toxic ways, the outside doctors the inside. This is evolutionary history and this is a metabolic response to the energy technologies of my historical moment. Petrochemicals brand hormonal messages that course through endocrine pathways and drive my metabolism. I wear multinational companies in my flesh. But I also wear symbiotic and parasitic relationships with countless nonhumans who insist for their own reasons on making me human. I want to know the stories of these chemicals, metals, and organisms that compose me. I am an event, a site within which the industrial powers and evolutionary pressures of my time come to write. I am a spectacular and horrifying crowd. How can I read me? How can I write me? I collect my blood, urine, sweat, and feces. I send them to laboratories to determine the levels and types of chemicals and microbes I find. I get tested for hundreds of substances that fall under the following groups: Phthalates, Dioxin-like chemicals, PCBS, PFCS, OCPS, PAHS, PBDES, HBCDS, Parabens, BPA, Triclosan, additional pesticides, and twenty-eight heavy metals. I also tune in to the signal of my microbiome by swabbing various areas of my body for bacteria – hand, genitals, ear, nose, and mouth. I obtain a deep metagenome and virome characterization of a stool sample, plus additional marker gene sequencing (16s rRNA, 18s rRNA and ITS) to characterize not just the bacteria but also the viruses, microbial eukaryotes, and fungi in my gut. I have some initial difficulty sending this sample across the border. I am a spectacular and horrifying assemblage. I resemble a battery. I wear uranium from well water in the Canadian Shield and

from the nuclear testing that marks me as a child of the Cold War. I
house bacterial colonies that have become empires of the Western
diet, fuelled by sugar, salt, and fat. I summon the energy to write by
way of a metabolism already written. What is inscribed in me is in
you, too.

## HORMONE

A few individuals
together

constitute
a crowd.

3 ppm of bromine,
500 ppm of benzene,

5 mg of arsenic,
500 colony-forming units

per millilitre
of tap water.

✳

In the sexual parts
of material history

every belief
has its crowd,

every crowd,
its medium.

✳

Some crowds
are slow
and wander
the wilderness.

It's not always the remoteness
of the goal
or the splendour
of the pilgrims.

Some include
every member
they've ever had
and ever will have.

One lifetime
reaches into
the next
like a sleeve.

Some crowds
accumulate
in the reproductive organs
of their maxims.

\*

Casseroles,
tea,
die-ins

at the stripmall
constituency office.
Fruit stand

vendor
on fire.
The crowd

is an accumulation
of what cannot
get out of the way.

*

Herd animals
were hunted
for food
but also
for the feeling
their numbers gave
the hunters.
Let there be more
of us, they prayed
and envied
the buffalo meat
that built railroads
and fuelled wagon trains.
Their hair was stuffed
into furniture. Shit
burned for heat.
Every nation
feels it is promised
the whole earth.
Every nation
sits atop
a pile
and waits.

*

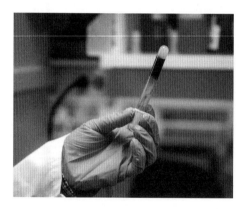

Adam, in order to test your body for the range of chemicals you have requested, you will need to send in approximately 62 mL of serum, equivalent to about 150 mL of whole blood, and approximately 6 mL of urine. Both the urine and serum should be sent in amber glass jars and cooled to below 4°C. Using the morning void would be best. There are no other restrictions besides making sure that the serum sample does not come into contact with any Teflon.

## AGENTS ORANGE, YELLOW, AND RED

*2,3,7,8-Tetrachlorodibenzodioxin (serum): 1.304348 pg/g lipid*

You are either for chlorine
or for the plague.
Right now is the cleanest
we have ever been, and for this
you must love aerial defoliants
or you love communism.
Under the bandage of this one-industry
town closing ranks around staples
of forestry and fish, the wound
is wide-eyed and headstrong.
Through the clearing, freshwater carp
blink past the graves of missionaries
who introduced them to the New World.
Northern rivers are warmed
by the paper mill's piss, which,
like making the world safe for democracy,
slowly leaked into my childhood, yellowing
the lipophilic paperbacks of my
adipose fat. You are for pulp
or for poverty. You respect
the Constitution or you stare
at the ground lost in bankruptcies
for herring gull beaks or blurred
embryos in cormorant colonies.
Every erected media platform reduces
the problem of war to a problem
of tint. During the Orange Revolution,
Viktor Yushchenko was poisoned
by government agents who haywired
his food with dioxin. His face flared
into pages of acne. You are either
for the red or the white blood cells,
for the tops of trees, or the bottoms.

I filled seventy-six vials of blood. The centrifuge I used would take only small tubes, which is why I needed so many. My veins were a mess. I took short breaks to walk around the room swinging my hands. By the end of it, I was drawing from both arms and yanking on the tourniquet with my teeth.

My generous assistant was not a trained phlebotomist. We did it during his free time at the university. The university eventually found out what we had done. New policies were put in place.

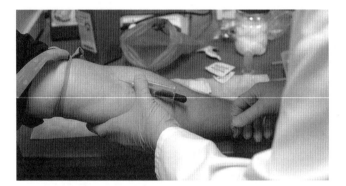

# FRUIT BELT

*Carbofuranphenol (urine): <0.1 ug/L*
*Dimethylphosphate (urine): 2.6 ug/L*
*4,4'-DDT (serum): 5.072464 ng/g lipid*

My wife and I cough differently. She leans into her sleeve, encouraging replacement leaders. I am less sanguine about stems and must cover my mouth during toasts. She is shade tolerant and takes her asthma for a run in ravines ravaged by dog-eared understories. I cough to test my inguinal narratives for spring on automated blossoms bearded with hair triggers. She coughs at the same time as applause, sensitive to the seedless struggle for dominance that defines our clingstone generation. I blow out birthday candles on other peoples' cakes. She is generous to a fault and cuts to the chase with a cocktail sword, hands on her hips like the last native variety pulled up by free trade. Post-nasal, I reverse into parking spaces, wiping out the element of surprise. Dry and persistent, she encrypts her skin with moisturizers. Cacophony is inflammation. The residue of every suppressant we've ever tried keeps bucking within us like a bronchus. We listen at night for the croup of airguns keeping the migratory birds from the orchards. Our girls sleep through it in the room next door.

## HORMONE

*

Fire
in a crowded theatre
is constrained
by free speech.
The more easily
a thing burns
the less it can defend
itself from freedom.
Each person
sees the door
through which
they may freely pass.
Frames punish
their pictures.
The same flames
give different versions
of resistance,
but the more
one has to say,
the more one is captive
to the ovens
joining together
what was separate
in the shortest
possible time.
Animals flee
the freedom of the forest
for the burning streets.
The arsonist lives
alone with the freely
associated details

of a confession.
Suppressed in one place
it rises in another,
the enemy of free spirits.
There is no escaping
the free world.
It surrounds us
like an aspirin
in a drink.
When it seems
crowded with fire,
the trampling
that accompanies panic
is just the urge
to stomp it out.

\*

It looked like I was going to have to shit in Buffalo. I needed to send a stool sample across the border and it would be easier to simply go to Buffalo, produce what needed to be produced, and send it from there. The problem was that it appeared I was going to need a significant amount – more than one sitting. And I would have to freeze it. I wasn't holding out much hope for a hotel room with a deep freezer. I weighed my options. Strange to spend a weekend in Buffalo with the sole purpose of collecting and mailing my poop. In the end, the paperwork came through and I carefully placed everything to harden in our basement freezer.

# GALACTIC ACID

*Lactobacillus acidophilus*

For the first two years of my life, my mother's vaginal flora lived in my stomach. Consigned to the edge of their star system, they ate everything I ate, fermenting chains of starch into acids that fed the high-energy demands of trying to erect an antenna. The flora flexed for deep space, convinced they weren't alone. They transmitted their contractions and hoped to reach aliens before the terrible facsimiles of the 1970s: humans drawn without sex organs and burdened by messages whose content had become instructions for reading. Set amidst this mucosa, a gram-stained parabolic reflector waited for word from newcomers. We're a lot alike, my mother and I. Our disdain for underachieving campsites and the way we signal for help by maintaining a slight underbite during awkward conversations. Her vagina made me cosmopolitan. A dialectic crowned in the forest, its many antlers have since come to crowd my self-possession with spent velvet. I watch my mother favour her disintegrating hips. The small party that left her for the new world founded a settlement on a moon she still tracks without looking. Its tidal pull on the pit of her stomach makes her pause at the zenith of a phone call: 'What is it?'

# HORMONE

*

Anxiety waits
for a table
under a cave painting.
Water stirred

with a spear.
Keeping it together
is a form of digestion,
and digestion

is a form of commitment
to the dignity
of letting it go.
One part of you,

as an act of survival,
starts eating another part.
This is a membranous
decision

in which the crowd,
having mistaken
its periphery, resembles
its prey.

It was unbearable
to see the possum
lying there.
You asked me

to drive over its head
with the car. Hope
is such a strange
evolutionary adaptation.

What selective pressures
must have been
its shepherd,
what drinking glass

with an envelope
placed over the top
carrying a spider outside?
Against the occupations

and desertions,
against the bodies
tied to trees
and the flags partitioning

the wind above them,
against the accumulated
wealth
that acquires a house

with an aquarium
big enough to require
its own diver,
against the majuscule

Idea of refined sugars
and depictions of capital
concentrating
on its breathing,

there is this hopeful
monster.
You breastfeed
the survivor

with coded plans
for escape.
The signal slips
through undetected

like the possum
and its adaptive
capacity
to convincingly die.

*

## MOUTHFEEL

*Catenibacterium mitsuokai*
*Bacteroides*

The tongue map
is wrong.
There are buds down

to the commonwealth.
What was the bliss
point of African blood

in the table sugars
of Europe?
Every year,

spinach produces
a sugar
in its leaves

comparable
to the world's
annual output

of iron ore.
Without hurting
the taste, a young child

can stand
to keep a hand
in cold water

longer
with a sweet mouth.
The faster starch

converts to Christianity,
the quicker each outreach
over police radios.

O my sweet tooth,
my oatmeal raisin,
my poisoned tipped

candy apple cart.
Pleasure from food
is the air waving goodbye

in heat,
distorted
like an inherited empire.

In this way,
we are closest
to people who touch

what we eat.
Captives of loneliness
stare into icing.

I know enough
about the cherry on top
to lick around the sides.

I had to keep a food diary before obtaining my stool sample. I had never paid such close attention to what I ate before. The Word-made-flesh of a sweet potato. The onion domes of Russia in the garlic bulb's imperial fibre. All those calories packed into a few grams of butter, a bowl of pasta. All those calories knitted into the harvesting and flatbeds, sewn delicately into the crop dusts and mists that make them inhospitable to the insects and fungi that are their first and most desirous admirers. If I ate less, I would limit the PCBs, pesticides, and metals that could get in, right? This idea consumed me.

## INTEGRATED PEST MANAGEMENT

*Aldrin (serum): 0.7391304 ng/g lipid*
*Chlordane, oxy- (serum): 7.681159 ng/g lipid*
*2,4'-DDD (serum): 0.7391304 ng/g lipid*

It is enzyme hour.
Front lawns part their hair,
waiting for instructions.
Fat kids run through
sprinklers with shirts on
over grass growing
shapelessly in the deciduous forests
of the large intestine.
With mid-century Manichaeism,
many a man has lusted
after Wrigley Field,
its pre-emptive stripes
against the perennial apologists
for divided cells.
Be alive
to your inner bowling green,
its role in the spread
of the horse, the wheel,
and the postwar
laboratory limb. Grass
climbs out of the limbic system
into changing climates
of sex, hunger, offspring care.
'Play outside,' my mother scolded.
I was fertilized by early cultivars
of pasteurized milk
and river muck
yolking my hands
with ventilated eagle eggs.
We hate the insects.

We hate them
under the streetlights
with their primitive foreshadows.
Our solution
is perfectly safe. When people
try to commit suicide by drinking it,
they fail regularly.

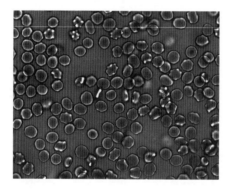

When the results started to arrive, I felt tense. A door was about to open into a mail-room filled with incommunicable antibodies strung from a bare wire. I read them quickly, not wanting to let my eyes linger on anything alarming. When I came across a chemical that measured among the top percentiles, I panicked. I felt sick. Cortisol dripped. Death comes like a letter that folds its recipients.

## Δ

Fat is an organ. It echoes with music and memory. Fat is a slowly oscillating wave. It embodies the constancy of transition, clinging as a perpetually updated fuel reserve, an accumulation expressing – through hourglasses, pears, and apples – the energy balance of a life being lived. Fat is a metaphysics conditioning experiences of reality. It regulates hormones and directs the transitional modalities of metabolic processes. Fat provides stability, padding, and insulation to equip a body in transition, moving through climates and calories, catastrophes and capitalism. Fat feeds us, but Western-style commerce has afflicted many parts of the world with obesity. Children are filled with accelerated derivatives of excavated sunlight and profitably supply-chained processed foods. Fat is an archive of this historical moment. Military, industrial, and agricultural history bioaccumulate in adipose tissues. I have found one of the most widely distributed environmental contaminants on the planet in my body: polychlorinated biphenyls, PCBs. Principally manufactured by Monsanto for industrial and commercial applications, these lipophilic pollutants collect like comment sections in the fat of creatures everywhere. If we test for them, we will find them. PCBs constitute a form of writing in the Anthropocene, a recursive script where industrial innovations find their way back into the metabolic messaging systems of the biological bodies that have created them. As edits, as subtle revisions to the hormonal cascades that precipitate bodily morphologies and affective experiences of the world, PCBs are messages in the fat of our humanity.

The first section of 'Lipids' appropriates language from *The Handwriting Analyst's Toolkit: Character and Personality Revealed through Graphology* by Peter West (New York: Barron's Educational Series, Inc., 2004.). Each of the eight stanzas successively treats the eight letters in the word 'Monsanto,' using language associated with the graphological analysis of each letter. Until it ceased production in 1977, Monsanto was the source of approximately 99 percent of the PCBs used by U.S. industries.

## LIPIDS

*Polychlorinated Biphenyls, # 105 (plasma): 1.88 ng/g lipid*

Angular
arches.
Inwardly curved,
short final stroke
compulsively avoids
responsibility.

Open top,
stabbed.
Two parts hypocrisy,
tight-fisted.
Loops in the oval,
deceptive.

Wide, wakefully
streaked.
Selfish with hands
inhibited
by persistent
tapering at reversal.

Watchful and hooked.
Start
with secretive
sharp tongues.
Selfish figures
arc or claw.

Whether right
or wrong,
emphatically squared.
Avaricious finish
at the double knot
gossip close.

Wide, wakefully
streaked.
Selfish with hands
inhibited
by persistent
tapering at reversal.

Split stem
whiplike
long bar
mimicry.
Self-protective
pressures disloyal.

Open top,
stabbed.
Two parts hypocrisy,
tight-fisted.
Loops in the oval,
deceptive.

When my mother's breasts were building my brain, her milk sent me a postcard from the postwar boom. The message was scrambled. Proprietary. Windborne elsewhere's outfall spikes. Face-swirled factories with disjunctive hair loss. Heat-waved skin. Malignant neoplasms of indefinite dose. Headquartered in the subtext were inscrutable companies conflicted with interest, like urban forests or chlorine, sending people to work under crumbling narrative arcs. Smoothing their loose-leaf, they made us believe we were victims of atmosphere. My jaw owes its plotlines to my mother's breasts, even as they've been ghost-written by power grids redesigning sensoria from a diaspora of unseasonal thunderheads. In a world that persists on bottles of cabin pressure, her milk beaded my lips with formulas.

*Polychlorinated Biphenyls, # 138 (plasma): 9.69 ng/g lipid*

prefatory
baby fat
fatal

milk fat
infatuate
fatigue

fat lip
butter fat
fat cheque

fatuous
forefathers
kill the fatted calf

fat as a beached whale
fat as a pig
the fat lady sings

chew the fat
fatherland
fatwa

fat chance
fatalist
fat fuck

indefatigable
fatuity
the fat is in the fire

unfathomed
blood fat
fat of the land

Before entering the Zone, the writer, the professor, and their guide fell asleep beside a river. The surface of the water was obese with lather. Waves slurred beneath a heavy blanket while a strong wind picked at the fire-extinguished foam. Tarkovsky filmed *Stalker* here near Tallinn, Estonia. A chemical plant emptied its effluent just upstream near a half-functioning hydroelectric station. Allergic reactions climbed the faces of the crew. Tarkovsky, his wife, Larisa, and actor Anatoly Solonitsyn all died from cancer of the right bronchial tube.

adhesives and tapes arrive

bushings arrive

cable insulation sets foot

capacitors set foot

carbonless copy paper muscles

caulking muscles

cork breaks in

electromagnets break in

felt worms

fibreglass worms

floor finish creeps

fluorescent light ballasts creep

foam insinuates

hydraulic oil insinuates

motor oil colonizes

oil-based paint colonizes

plastics horn

switches horn

transformers leak

transformers leak

In Aamjiwnaang First Nation, only a third of all babies are boys. The hockey team has disbanded. Girls' softball was added. Refineries rim the community with pipes. Cholera, smallpox, the British, and the French split piles of young Anishinabek men. In unceded lipidscapes, offspring now flare with feedback. Injuries take their course like conclusions draw baths. Boilerplates rust in jurisdictional prudence. On the back of the old ten-dollar bill, the picture of smokestacks and holding tanks could only have been taken by standing on the reserve. I called to ask.

The real star
is the food.
It's attached
to every
period theme,
slicing through
herbivores
and spinach dip
with the heartburn
of a meteor.
Trenchant
and toothsome,
huge platters of fowl.
The taste excuses
representational
behaviour,
but every crater
in the mouth
is a landing pad
for the unmanned
messianism
of hormones.
It's so obvious
in the face
and neck
that choice
means more often
superior.
Nostalgia
for the first bite
of prepared
predator.

Heat hangs
sentimentally
in the electrical
grid's unpublished
correspondence,
abbreviated
by unreliable
litters of pack ice.
Feel the taste of it.
What makes them
so attractive
makes them hard
to destroy.

My gut is a tropical forest of microbes. Their cells, which cover my entire body, are at least as numerous as my own. These microbiota live on and within me as a giant nonhuman organ, controlling the expression of genes and the imagined sense of self maintained by my immune system's sensitivity to inside and outside. It is unclear, in fact, whether the immune system controls the microbes or the microbes control the immune system. My body is a spaceship designed to optimize the proliferation and growth of its microbial cosmonauts. These organisms enact a form of biochemical writing through their integral involvement in the metabolic processes that fuel my life. In some cases, the proliferation of certain species can improve the health of the host. The oligosaccharides in honey, for example, which are indigestible to humans, can stimulate the growth of *Bifidobacteria* in my gut, potentially reducing the risk of food allergies and colonization by pathogens. The enzyme *beta-fructofuranosidase* from *Bifidobacterium longum* is one such catalyst for handling the oligosaccharides from honey in the anaerobic environment of my large intestine.

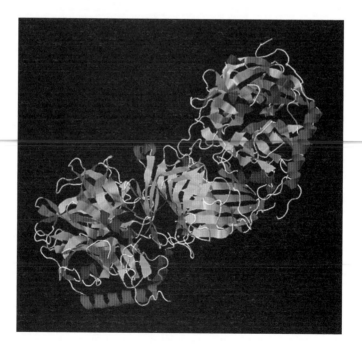

1 *mtdftpetpv ltpirdhaae lakaeagvae maakrnnrwy pkyhiasngg windpnglcf*
61 *ykglwhvfyq lhpygtqwgp mhwghvsstd mlswkrepim fapsleqekd gvfsgsavid*
121 *dngdlrfyyt ghrwanghdn tggdwqvqmt alpdndelts atkqgmiidc ptdkvdhhyr*
181 *dpkvwktgdt wymtfgvssa dkrgqmwlfs skdmvrweye rvlfqhpdpd vfmlecpdff*
241 *pikdkdgnek wvigfsamgs kpsgfmnrnv snagymigtw epggefkpet efrlwdcghn*
301 *yyapqsfnvd grqivygwms pfvqpipmed dgwcgqltlp reitlgddgd vvtapvaeme*
361 *glredtldhg sitldmdgeq iiaddaeave iemtidlaas taeraglkih atedgaytyv*
421 *ayddqigrvv vdrqamangd rgyraapltd aelasgkldl rvfvdrgsve vyvngghqvl*
481 *ssysyasegp raiklvaesg slkvdslklh hmksigle*

Saliva is disorganized
and easily fooled by success.
It's not even true
that I eat honey.
Within the province of drive-thrus
and sleeper cells,
something else does it for me,
stuffing aspartame briefcases
with municipal snow.
At the business end of this shit,
complex sugars are abducted
by aliens necktied
in a carpool, still rocking
classic haircuts and metabolic
pathways from the oxygen-starved
oceans of Archean Earth.
I don't have to move a muscle.
*Bifidobacteria* break down the best
defence and special teams,
build welfare states
and a culture of dependence
also found in hamster dental plaque,
Mongolian fermented horse cream,
pig intestines, and honeybee

digestive tracts. The limits
of my enzymes
mean the limits of my world.
Milk and honey
curd a landscape as pointless
as a fingerprint.
In the prehistory of the gut,
getting off this planet
means getting someone else
to take the wheel.

*Methylophilaceae*

Amber shared a wing. It was in her mouth. She had killed a bird and laid part of it on our steps. Amber was a Saint Bernard crossed with a Ridgeback crossed with a switchblade. Her prey-drive always circled several times before lying down. Mice, moles, rabbits. She riffled through their bodies like evidence, delivering them to us as wilted envelopes through the information services of her soft-faced mouth.

We got her after one of my dad's friends joined the military. She roamed the neighbourhood like a keyboard; dogs wandered as fluently as children through the folksongs of a parenting style in which helicopters had long since left the embassy rooftops. We never tied her up.

Mr. Langston didn't want her on his property. Mr. Langston was a prospector and he wasn't home very often, but when he was, he lived between our houses like a boulder. His huge travelling packs were filled with salted pork, axes, and dynamite. We could see the fuses. He had been dropped into our world by a glacier from another century. Cobalt, uranium, nickel, and gold.

Mr. Langston lived alone. His only companion was a cat whose fur was abandoning its body. It crept about with the nudity of a washed hand. Our young lives, conversely, were crowded with insurgent flags like autumn leaves in a storm drain. We had insatiable appetites for the internal provinces of absorption. Every scrape we acquired was an opportunity to peel another scab, to pull back the blankets and watch the wound bed dream. We crowded into Mr. Langston's loneliness with our freehand markets, peddling improbable stories about caves full of gold leaf guarded by bears with fangs like liberty spikes.

My friend Luke said we should sneak into his house. You could tell when Luke was serious because he'd start licking his lips, and they'd shine back at you when he was talking. Mr. Langston's house was known to us only in the brief moments when we accompanied our parents to drop off food or hold the door as they helped him through the prism of holiday drinks. Sometimes the drinks made him chase us. We were warned to stay off his property. He kicked me once so hard and so surprisingly I nearly bit through my lip. For days I ran my tongue over the contour of the wound rhythmically and obsessively. It took a long time to heal. We stopped cutting across his lawn. Instead, we used the street, with its rooster-tailed stones.

Inside his house was the inside of an idea whose minerals were as obscure to us as the geodes posing vaginally by the woodstove, their crystals glistening inward. Clocks ticked with the wrong times. Windows were shaded with the climatological stratus of cigarette smoke. His house smelled like someone had been bankrolling soil, floating its reclamation mission with unambiguous faith. It was obvious that the man ate nothing but dirt. That's how you looked for metals. You had to eat the dirt to know what was in it.

It didn't take long for us to find the bucket. Some things take longer than others to appear, but we were always on the lookout for outlines, stains, relief, for swellings amidst no obvious injury. Like Amber, who, in broad daylight, once attacked the moving wheels of my dad's truck. An ambush we respected, if only for its resolute commitment to the interiority of a circulatory system similarly beyond our reach.

Under the sink, beside the vinegar and empty wine bottles with corks jammed back into their necks, was a giant plastic bucket. It was enormous, the kind of pail used to haul field-dressed deer parts, or brimmed with salt at the curbside crosswalks in town. It looked like the kind of bucket my mom had me fill with ashes from the furnace to take out to the compost. If there was snow, I usually set the bucket down without emptying it and let it melt its way to the ground.

We thought it was pine pitch, or chicken fat, but it was honey. Deep almost-burnt amber, it consumed every calorie of the stark kitchen light. Prehistoric insects with their arms folded were preserved in its depths; a few cat hairs were spider-legged on top. He kept honey in the subatomic loneliness of his mid-latitude bungalow. We cupped it with our fingers and then our hands. Our faces glistened. Strands of it returned to earth on trajectories mathematically determined by our rolled-back eyes. We crammed it into our mouths with slurred speech, this strange moonlight reflected from the planetary face of a defenceless animal on its back barely breathing as we ate its entrails. The plasma glistened on our lips.

In retrospect, how could he not return to find us there? We were populists imposing our assembled convictions on the conspicuous eccentric. We were vigilantes storming the castle in the name of nothing but burlesque. Such indiscretions inevitably receive the face of their target the way the crowd moves through streets only to become the streets themselves, scraping glass loose from storefronts, awakened. When we heard him at the door and finally saw him, we tried to make it out the back, but our legs barely moved. He stood there with his hands apart. His mouth was open, but he didn't say anything. He smelled like dirt to us, like an overturned rock revealing its clandestine cities of spiders and earthworms, collaborating all this time on an elaborate resistance to the world as we knew it.

We drained from his house like syrup and collapsed on the safe side of the property line. My mother shrieked as she came outside. She had her arms bent at the elbows and her fingers spread like she did when she was handling meat. 'Oh, my god,' she said. 'You'd better go home.'

Not long after we were made to apologize, I saw Mr. Langston in his yard chopping wood. Each piece stood before him in the form of a confession. They all ended the same way. He paused for a moment to look over at me when something caught his attention. Amber was in the bushes at the back of his property, her body hovering, snapping branches as she twisted. Before I could call her, she emerged. Mr.

Langston stared at her. I waited for him to lift his axe, but he stood there like a piece of his own wood. She bounded toward me with something in her mouth. She dropped the limp cat at my feet. Its hairlessness was shocking. Here was a body whose skin was hunting down and killing its own coat, follicle by follicle. It made me shiver not to think of it.

## HORMONE

*

The unconscious
is structured
like a hormone.

The ideas of the past
are already quorum sensing
the ideas that will replace them.

*

A hormone conjugates its subject. First, a stimulus. It could be glucose in the blood, it could be the pervasive, uncontrollable fear of being poisoned. A sequence of events is set in motion. Insulin is produced to handle sugar. Sugar is made available to the blood. Either way, I'm taking a deep dive into my own bodily fluids to try and read them. But the pool is an empty helmet. My magnified blood cells. My dark mirror stage.

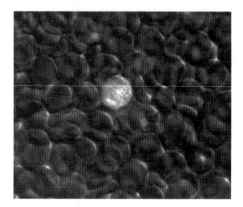

## HORMONE

*

At the centre
of every crowd
is a ladder.
Both criminal
and hero ascend
into fugitive impulses
long civilized out
of any one individual
but kept alive
in the deforming action
of an obsessive thought.
A glitterpath forms
in the red end
of its parent light.
Slogans share mouths
with rivers and jars.
There is never a time
we are not being fed.
I'm wearing a striped shirt.
I'm at the back
by the railing.
If you see me
it is because the crowd
has already left the party
and is now
stoning the host.
I am standing
on stones.

*

## OCD

We ran into the police escort east of Nipigon. Cars sat undigested along the roadside. He jogged toward us on his prosthetic leg, part hop, part kite, part fire escape. His fists were clenched and his elbows locked, carrying a stack of dictionaries to safety before a speechless crowd stunned in the broken wrist of a rock cut. Nobody said a word. Engines idled while his footsteps typefaced the centre line. Silence swallowed its spit. The cancer had come back. Everyone was crying in the simplest sugars, so nothing made it beyond a single mouth before falling apart. A four-year-old girl with a big grin finally shouted, 'Hi, Terry!' It was the only sound for a thousand kilometres. 'Hi,' he said back softly to my sister. Sweat squinted from his body, looking out at us from the liquid crystal of his guts. For months afterwards, I obsessively practiced his gait. I held my fists before me and pulled my body as a sequence of events over shifting centres of gravity. How does one life live inside another? When does it try to get out?

I started scrutinizing my body. I watched it for abridged exit rows. My right eye was tear shade. Tired of eating. I tested each morsel for numbness. I performed ritualistic experiments on my sense of cumulative contour. Tried walking the centre lines of roads clover-leafed with anti-vaxxer headlights belittling my eyesight. Headed off to see the head-ons, I was the mademoiselle of the gazelles. I slurred my words, saying this alone in a dark legume. The count. It got late in my ribcage and birds landed to pick my brain out of the clamshell takeouts sexed with houseflies. The guy who brings his own lamp to the archives is not fucking around. The guy who finds his archive filled with lamps is terrified of his burglarized flesh. The lights were on the whole time.

## CIRCULATION

Staphylococcus

If they worked together, the microbes could eat us in a few days. Our bodies would blacken, liquefy, and run into the streets. I keep thinking I can feel them, and so I wash my hands of their stop-motion ponds. Anxiety is a form of autoimmunity. You can't be trusted with your own intentions. I wash my hands and then I think to wash my hands. This is an attempt at silence. Sterile palms hold forth with little more than the hardiest *Staph*. I am on the windward side of a dialectic built from idiolects and sweat. Take me to the fire-wood to live with the trees.

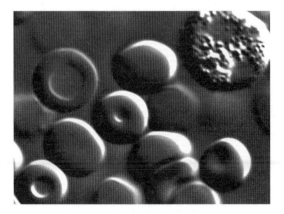

I began to make excuses for walking. I walked everywhere, even when I had nowhere to go. Some days, I would walk over twenty kilometres. I know because I started keeping track. I felt calm when I was walking. The anxiety temporarily diminished. I sensed the functional reality of exertion, my metabolism burning calories into heat, sending smoke puffing out the slacked chimney of my mouth. I wasn't dying when I was breathing this heavily. In and out. Nothing stayed for long. I wasn't anywhere. A cloud.

## IT TURNS OUT THE STARTING MATERIAL FOR THE EARLIEST FORMS OF LIFE IS A CARCINOGEN

*1-Hydroxybenz(a)anthracene (urine): <0.002 ug/L*
*1-Hydroxyphenanthrene (urine): 3.9 ug/L*
*1-Hydroxypyrene (urine): 6 ug/L*

Hash with a dime
in a beer bottle.
Burning defines me
like froth
at the corkscrew of an argument
over the illusion of safety.
My compulsions
are all monuments
to incomplete combustion,
by which I mean particulate
matters compromise my unmanned
willingness for nerve endings.
I wear smoke immunologically
like a barrel with suspenders
or well-heeled neighbourhoods
with street associations
taking care of quiet boulevards
like cottage-country lakes.
Suspended in the water column,
fish hearts slow to the length
of time it takes the marinade
to soak in. Diesel rigs run all night
at the truck-stop diner
amidst the alphabetic disparity
between benzene rings and highway signs
buckshot by glitched-up guano.
Hitchhikers may be escaped
inmates. Things make
sense more easily

if they are attached to moods.
Every night I replay
the half-baked getaway
of a running nose,
trying out cigarettes and accelerants
on cuts of meat.

I lost about eighteen kilograms of weight. This meant I had to buy new clothes. I was determined to starve the chemicals out of my fat and deprive the microbes of their sugar highs. I was feeling like shit and took it out on the people closest to me.

## HORMONE

✳

We are on our way
to the hospital
to free the germs.
As with any siege,
partisans beg to be let in.
As long as the traitor
is quiet, the crowd
lets him eat and drink
and make love.
Unless a sense of justice
can weigh its own compromise,
it will eventually succumb
to its scales.
Some of us are standing
in the water feature
evolving
out of the situation.
Kidneys rinse and fold
their blood supplies.
Glucose sits poised
like a mallet
over glass.

✳

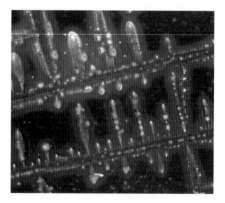

My tests tell me I have a lower capacity for breaking down certain large-branched sugars. This can promote infection. But I also have lower gene counts for endotoxin, which may mean less inflammation.

All I hear is infection. I feel stuffed to the brim. I am breathing only at the very end of each breath. Anxiety is taxidermy animated by the insides of something else's guts.

## A STRING OF SMALL PEARLS

*Group A Streptococcus*

Now we are in the throat.
Necks

are the hardest animal
parts to scale.

We are in the throat,
disingenuous

with the night-time sleeping
arrangements for ulcers.

Now we are in the throat
as the caterpillar

and butterfly parent
completely partitioned worlds.

We prick light
on a throat

culture
of entitlement, remarkable

for its moth-eaten,
tonsillar birthright.

Hospitals are being infected
by their inhabitants'

throats.
We are in the throat

throwing
the security forces

off our scent.
Insurrection

is metabolism practiced
with spit.

We are in the throat,
sharing the same spoon.

# HORMONE

*

Beyond the social forces
that influence them,
crowds

are guided
by their dead.
They off-gas

from synthetic furniture
in hotel rooms
with the low-amplitude hum

of a spaceship
idling in the dark
near the Tannhäuser Gate.

The outside world
has been
destroyed

and watercolour
sailing regattas
are the new spores.

*

My children occupy the campground with their unfinished bodies. I should be relaxing, but I'm a circus tent soft-served with vertigo. The sunshine is sliced to pieces on the handlebars and spiral slides. Is it possible to say that in fucking me up, the chemicals exalt me? Vanadium. Manganese. What the hell? How much exhaust have I been sucking?

## THE PEOPLE OF GRASSY DON'T HAVE A MERCURY PROBLEM, THEY HAVE A DRINKING PROBLEM

*Mercury (blood): 1.42 ug/L*

They were no longer themselves and there was talk of making a national park to solve the problem. This kind of talk was the part of the problem where the problem people are spread onto maps and folded into animal shapes on long car trips through the wilderness. There was talk of the problem in a few arms and legs that couldn't talk and so folded in on each other and clenched on something no one could see, which seemed heartbreaking and unnecessary but was a way of signalling that the problem was all around us, that the problem could be touched and when touched it would grab back like the rapids in that river. There was talk that the waters were not polluted, and if they were polluted, then the company was not responsible. There was talk that nothing escaped from the plant, and if anything did escape, the company did not know it was harmful. There was talk that bodies were not actually poisoned, and if they were poisoned it was because of what goes into them, the weekends in Kenora, the altered dream-states that break into leaf in this culture, but culture urine and vomit in the streets of that culture. There was talk that they couldn't hold their liquor, as if liquor were a front door you held open for a crowd pouring in to pound your liquor. The fur trade was in there burning in a shooter. There was talk about how drinking was one long peristaltic protest against colonialism, an attempt to clear the throat as perfectly good protein threw itself into rivers, through car windshields. Some people went on talking like this. And here I have it in my blood talking, a settler methylated by the privilege afforded by the problem's extremities shaking with poorly connected dreams. All this talking and I am beginning to repeat myself. Myself.

I'm a white male. My body is marked by certain demographic privileges. It is true that racism and economic marginalization can cause people to live in closer proximity to industrial pollution. It is also true that privilege, with its associated dietary and hygiene opportunities, can lead to a less diverse microbiome and increased incidence of gut infections. This is especially true on a global scale, where citizens of disadvantaged regions often have much more diverse microbiomes and fewer immune-related illnesses than their wealthier neighbours. The chemicals and microbial signatures may be different for distinct communities of people, but the chemicals and microbes are in us all.

# A MINOR EXCRETORY ORGAN

*Lead (blood): 1.36 ug/dL*

It's easy to feel detached. But it's easy to eat someone else's stray hair in a salad. This is globalization. You can raise a glass of water to adulthood, confident you've done everything right, but still the companies are counting on us to love that part of ourselves that is them. One way to solve a complicated problem is to endure a smaller version of the same problem. The carousel was sourced from Toronto's Sunnyside Park, but Disney wanted only galloping horses, so their legs were broken and the horses refitted. Collections of baby teeth were started in 1958 to measure levels of strontium-90 in people living near nuclear plants. When the king gave a single strand of hair, or let his hair be touched, his courtiers knew he had just paid them his most valued compliment.

I became competitive with myself over caloric deficits. 500, 1000, 1500. It was hard to concentrate some days and I was sure I was slurring my words. I asked other people if they noticed anything. I didn't believe them if they hadn't. I had to stop reading Ben Lerner's *10:04* because it made me feel I was at risk of an impending aortic dissection. I was dizzy. I felt tingling in my arms and legs and was sent for an MRI. I underwent a colonoscopy after complaining of digestive problems. There was a complication with the procedure and a week later, after a poetry reading, I went back to the hotel and shat a toilet bowl full of blood. I was in the hospital for two days and anemic for many months. Sometimes even walking couldn't quiet the obsessive thoughts. The doors I locked, and locked again, opened behind my back. When I was a kid, one of my testicles went up inside my body for a while. I became convinced this was the result of my exposure to chemicals. The chemical tests had put my body under surveillance, but it was watching me watch it. I was living my life like a splinter being slowly driven into my own skin.

# BY ALL MEANS, SURE, CERTAINLY, ABSOLUTELY

*Arsenic (blood): 11 nmol/L*

The actor who played the gravedigger was my friend's father. After his parents split, we'd cut class to deal stud in his mother's basement. My first time voting was in the Charlottetown referendum, a consti-tutional bed skirt hung out to dry like poorly laundered regionalism. When my friend's father showed up at the polling station without ID, I vouched for him, though I wondered why he'd driven there without a licence. During the summer, I piled wood at the mill, filled orders, and hid behind the hemlock lifts by the river smoking menthols. He would show up occasionally in a small dented pickup looking for plywood and strapping. The community theatre was building one last set before the festival went underwater. Deficit hawks were dive-bombing the new vanishing points of civil expediency and I started to believe that the pits of Ontario peaches had arsenic in them. As it turns out, 100 g of peach seed contains 88 mg of cyanide. The arsenic was in the pressure-treated lumber I cut and stacked every day. The sawdust smelled of a fresh deck of cards. It hung in the air near the radial arm saw like a biography unable to hold narrative coherence, like a dream protecting sleep by making everything familiar.

There are no safe levels of any of the chemicals I was tested for. What's a safe level? What's an adverse effect? Industry welcomes the imposition of guidelines because this would give them permission to pollute people up to a line with impunity. Our bodies are adaptive, but in adapting they change and those changes can affect the ability to undertake other functions. People have widely varying sensitivities. A small additional challenge can push someone over a tipping point to sickness, even if many others are not measurably harmed. What's a safe level? What's an adverse effect?

*Cadmium (blood): 0.13 ug/L*
*Cobalt (blood): 0.20 ug/L*

Doug kept a wedge of Limburger cheese in the rafters of the saw shed. He liked the smell of feet. Mark shot a bear and brought the roasted meat for lunch. He had been to jail for sixty days after trying to steal a lawnmower. His drunken, slow-motion getaway from the Rent-All on Main Street was a nightcap turned tranquilizer dart and was on the third page of the local newspaper. After I went back to school in the fall, Mark showed up at my house late one afternoon in tears. He couldn't think straight, he said. 'Nobody gets me.' Hopelessness is a transition metal in mammals. Wayne was our boss and sat high in the forklift all day moving pallets of cedar and fir and spruce. He teased Mark and Mark took it like mucus. Diesel smoke belched from the forklift stack like after-dinner farts at the hunt camp. Don't-be-such-a-fag was the one stable isotope of the yard. Anne was Ojibwe and didn't take shit from any of them. But there was a lot of shit. Doug's cheese smelled like it. It was my job to keep a lookout for customers. We'd drink in the saw shed and give each other advice on how not to be assholes. Wayne's forklift idled just outside the door. The fumes sunk their metals in our blood like coins into a meter.

## HORMONE

*

Corn is so obedient
it can't conceive.
Resisting
a forest
internalizing
grass.
When cut,
it's a death
as equal as
a union town.
It towers over
its masters
like a haircut
killed midway
between abilities
to straighten itself.
One person, one vote.
Keep off the grass
and let the markets open
the genital tracts
of frogs.
One country, one flag.
A chicken in every pot
and a car
in every applause.
Doesn't take much
to make the corn
admit to everything.
Monsanto built
an empire
laying eggs

in heirlooms.
All the acorns
have old-timer's disease.
I can't say
a word you are saying.
Corn dogs
bark
through the night.

*

*Alistipes*
*Bacillus*
*Escherichia coli*

We punk-rocked our brains out that summer. What happens in the vagus nerve never stays in the vagus nerve. Each gig fattened in my head until the fleshy part was a pamphleteer pacing dietary fibre for grassroots. I think of you in my hippocampus college fingerpicking through memory stacks, setting neuron fires for warmth, like the first time I burned down a carb load eating asteroid ice at the axon of a guitar lick. Since then, new instruments come easily with prefrontal abandon, while the alien abductions I faked to lure you back are bandshells of their former selves. Perfect recall is really a spotlight into an energy drink too acrylic for reproduction. Come watch renal lobes filter copyright infringements. Ladies and gentlemen, I call this piece *Probiotic*. I know it like the back of a bottle of Molotov cocktail, like I know the military invented teenagers with baby booms. Smash the state! Smash it to bits. Take it home in a headache.

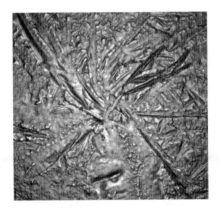

Walking was becoming its own form of dependence. I would pretend I wasn't going even when I was. If I had a large meal, I would walk late that night, after everyone else was in bed. Over the surface of a world whose merchandise circulates within my cellular respiration, each exhale was injuring the air. I didn't consent to carrying these chemicals inside me. I walked until I couldn't see stars.

Hormones have their own poetics. Secreted into the circulatory system in response to chemical signals, hormones write to distant organs. Their task is the prosody of metabolism – cellular rhythms harvest energy from food and air to fuel digestion, reproduction, growth, and the general health of a body. This book of glands and hormones makes up the endocrine system, an enduring evolutionary adaptation that has changed little in millions of years. Estrogen and its receptors are ancient, having continued for eons to perform important functions in all vertebrates and even in some insects. The hormone and its receptor fit together like a head into hands, or a hack into a password. The emergence of petrochemicals in the Anthropocene has coincided with the proliferation of endocrine-disrupting chemicals. These hormonal mimics, present in many common consumer products, are mistaken for keys to cellular locks, altering the body's hormonal chemistry. Phytoestrogens, abundant in many of the plants we eat, are also estrogen mimics; however, they are familiar antagonists in the long history of evolution – they are a defence mechanism against grazing. Plant estrogens lack the unprecedented potency of emerging chemicals such as phthalates. Phthalates are in everything from personal-care products, medical devices, and food packaging, to children's toys, air fresheners, and building materials. They are added to plastics to make them soft and pliable, to cosmetics as a lubricant and penetrant, and to fragrances and other scented products to increase the longevity of smells. The characteristic and desirable 'new car smell' is composed in part of phthalates off-gassing from plastic finishes. As estrogen mimics, phthalates can adversely affect the development of the reproductive system in mammals. They have been linked to infertility, lowered sperm counts, various reproductive tract malformations, asthma, obesity, and cancer, among other toxic effects.

*Mono-n-methyl phthalate (urine): 1.43 ng/mL*

The softness of phthalates is the softness of squeeze toys, pacifiers, and laboratory tubes. It's the softness of euphemisms eating dandelions by the roots. The radio smell of bug spray is as soft as a shower curtain taped to a car's missing window. Rules are made by those who enforce them. Soft power sits at the table like a soft drink. Soft-wood from Balsa trees is preferred for tables and chairs designed to splinter onstage in the theatre. During intermission, those who don't want to be there – having come to please someone, to smooth something over – smoke outside on the steps. They pretend to read calendars on their cigarette packs. The softness of phthalates is the softness of transparent packaging crumpled in a fist. When released it springs outward from memory.

cense
cents
scents
sense

cite
cyte
sight
site

medal
meddle
metal
mettle

rhos
roes
rose
rows

right
rite
wright
write

The young men are laughing as they enjoy having the bodies of men. At the hotel pool bar they pollinate each other with urine containing microscopic pieces of their own skeletons. Free testosterone circulates within them like motor oil making rainbows in the heads of parking spaces. They are not women. Say otherwise and they will fight you. They will fight you wearing aftershave and cologne. They will come at you through mousse and gearshifts, steering wheels and air fresheners, through fragrances, hair gels, and blood bags. They will advance on you through stabilized rubbers and resins, including nitrocellulose and polyvinyl acetates, soft gloves, jelly vibrators, and pvc pants. They will take you through slow dermal exposure, through their corresponding monoesters in the gastrointestinal tract, through excreted metabolites in their piss. They will kick your ass through androgen receptors and blocked endogenous hormones causing urogenital malformations. They will fight you. And they will shout down testicular dysgenesis! Down hypospadias! Down cryptorchidism! They will be sweating now and you will hardly recognize them, holding their limp bathing towels as industry lobbyists try to rally fishermen against chemical bans by telling them they will lose their flexible worms. The young men are glistening with sweat that comes out of them like browsing history. The things they touch touch them back, leaving small oil slicks inside that throw up colour wheels in the signals to their glands. They are not women. They will fight you. They believe this with the narrative authority of an intravenous drip.

*Monobenzyl phthalate (urine): 4.63 ng/mL*

The key
in pinkeye
and hand
in merchandise
and tongue
in cheek
and screw
in bolt and butter
in scotch
and coffee
in cups and
dinner in the bell
and periods
in the reasons
enumerated
for failure
and the fly's
field of vision
in the width
of the web
and the tick
in the sweat gland
horses
in the power
and the guest
in the host
and the knock
at the door
and the grammar
of the dancing
reproductive

success
of the bee
in the pollen
and the allergen's
revolt deciding
inside from out
and the shout
in the rooftop
and the drift
in the gene
and the spray
that comes in
from the crops
and the air
in the vent
and the vent
in the small hours
after damage
has been spent
and weeping
in the willow
and empire
in the fiddle
and Balkan
in the powder
and dark horses
in the running
and the absence
of questions
in the wandering
lust
and the fire
in the pinecone
and the halo
by virtues

of passion
in the fruits
with substrates
in the enzyme
and penis
in vagina
and the hetero
in normativity's
reflexive
complementarity
and floor tiles
in the embryo
and raincoats
in testicles
and the call
in the response
and the response
in the mouth
that makes the call

Under pressure to be fearless, the male brain sweats in a jar. The two halves are drawing different conclusions. How are other people feeling? The male brain thumbs tacks. Having been doused in an embryo at the buzzer, the male brain wanders into problems with a backpack full of explosives. Every night a pilot light schools its flagellant arms race, annealing metals in its dismounted police. Having bravely stood in a javelin rain, the male brain turns a blow dryer on a friend's stream of pee. Though it will never admit to this, the male brain is tense that its tense is the future perfect: what will have been the means by which it means? It squats in its skull like a cork.

*Mono-(2-ethyl-5-oxohexyl) phthalate (urine):  4.55 ng/mL*

I will not
let go
of your hand.

No, I
will not
let go

of your
hand.
No matter

what,
I've got
you.

Feel my
hand,
I've got

you.

*Mono-(2-ethyl-5-hydroxyhexyl) phthalate (urine): 5.37 ng/mL*

Phthalates light small scented candles for explorers who have just arrived on this peninsula and are now inquiring after its name. The locals tell them they don't understand the question. The visitors repeat, 'We do not understand the question,' with great difficulty pronouncing each word. 'We. Do. Not. Understand. The. Question,' they say over and over, lifting the backs of their tongues. At the meal held in their honour, the newcomers propose a toast. 'We do not understand the question,' they declare and point to the coast, their arms encircling the air above their heads, the backlit clouds, the smell of food and candles. We Do Not Understand the Question.

Grasses defend themselves.
Succulents defend themselves.
In an ordinary field, spines
and thorns. Foraged plants

defend themselves. Tannins,
terpenes, alkaloids. Difficulty
ripping and swallowing. Shrubs
have molecules dedicated

to bitterness. Some spike dead
stems to stop grazing. Some
suppress fertility in animals
that feed on them. Estrogen

mimics in phenolic rings. Beet,
barley, sunflower, rapeseed defend
themselves. Greeks and Romans
ate pine and pomegranate

to prevent pregnancy. Wheat,
sage, alfalfa, clover, soybean,
garlic, and hollyhock defend themselves.
Estradiol in the pill, phytoestrogens

in apples, bluegrass, oats, cherries,
rice, and rye. Plants defend themselves.
Dead plants defend themselves
rearranged into plastics. Estrogens

in air fresheners, shower curtains,
detergents, cosmetics. Estrogens
in water bottles, flame retardants,
children's toys, money. Estrogens

coat hands holding receipts.
Estrogens accumulate like sensible
heat. Date palm, rhubarb, willow
defend themselves. Plum, potato,

parsley defend themselves. Coffees
defend themselves with contraceptives.
In the beans, in the Mesozoic algae
in the disposable cup.

Cardboard coconut hanging from a string in a real estate agent's unventilated office. Pine tree in the cab of a half-ton humid with take-out. Little rose bouquet in a burned-out bathroom off the meeting rooms for a climate-change conference in Medicine Hat. Try to place the chemically manufactured smell of fruits and flowers and you find yourself on a debris flow into the uncanny valley. Like the creepy there's-a-knife-missing smile of those alert, oversized vinyl dolls for children, synthetic *Mango* is an overly macheted smell, too rigidly insistent on narrowly defined versions of vacation sex and culturally appropriated tropical breezes. *Aloe Blossom* is almost certainly an assassination attempt. It never succeeds, of course, because it emanates too much performance anxiety, gives away the game by forgetting to flick its ash. *Pumpkin Spice* is like hugging your grandmother, inhaling deeply, only to feel some of the stuffing emerge from the crease in her neck. Real fruit smells are handwritten notes soaked with sweat and read by the light of a flesh wound. They announce depth of desire, ripeness to act, and cultivated memories built out of carefully lit sugars. Synthetic fragrances barely recall anything except our untimely deaths at the hands of uniformed interiors in which every recollection becomes a plastic spoon wearing a mouthful of canned laughter. They appear in our cells like crayons misshapen and melted to the seat of a car parked in the sun.

## HORMONE

For many centuries
the crowd
concerned itself
with the crowd-sized world.

It eventually made it
to the moon
and looked back.
A different kettle of fish

appeared stranded
between sexes.
Identities are performed
and configured

according to the reiterative
power of bottles
to produce shrunken,
captured ships.

*

# YOU MIGHT NOT THINK THAT YOU DO THIS, BUT YOU DO

*Proprionibacterium*

A young Bill Clinton waited in line until the very last minute before lifting his hand. Forced to take a step forward, President Kennedy faced him squarely through the crowd of American Legion boys. Alexey Leonov used his strong grip to bleed air from a distended spacesuit. Having crash-landed soon after in Siberian snow, he hid from wolves in the broken capsule for two nights, emerging to greet his rescuers with hands warmed in his crotch. Jean Chrétien practiced the Shawinigan Handshake on the throats of hecklers. The night of the second Québec referendum, I was pushed against him on Parliament Hill. His gloved hand made my eyes water with its vinegar stink. When Kim Jong-il shook your hand, you knew you were loved. He practiced strenuously, injecting members of his staff with painkillers. All available photographic evidence suggests Margaret Thatcher offered Nelson Mandela a boiled sparrow shortly after his release from prison. When it's cold, I wipe blood on other people. A jackknife folded into my thumb years ago camping. I was carving a whistle. Cleaning myself in the lake, leeches arrived as lips jawlessly pursing in the digital weeds. Winters, the wound opens its fly, dry skin splitting along the scar seam, blood spotting my grip like electoral ink. The unfinished whistle appears with its primitive signal, the unconscious urge among people who shake hands to bring those shaken hands to their noses and mouths to smell them.

**HORMONE**

✳

A crowd with
little fingers
coming out of a stem.
They're fine.
My suitcases
are normal scores.
One
supporter
got up
and said,
'You have strong
clouds. You have
good-sized
blots.' And
another
would say,
'You have
a great surge,
I had no idea.
I thought
you were
deformed,
I thought
you had small
cattle.'
I mean, people
were writing,
'How are his droves?'
My clusters
are fine.

You know,
my bottlenecks
are normal.
Slightly large,
actually.
But I did
this because
everybody
was saying to me, 'Oh,
your parties
are very nice.'
They're normal.
But one of the things
he said was,
'You have a small
community
and therefore
a small
something else.'
There are
so many baskets
that nobody
writes about.
It's incredible.

*

Adam, cancer is an end point. Generally, there are many or different end points associated with any given compound. Because most of the compounds are found in the vast majority of the general population, it is important that the participant understand what they are being tested for and are tested with appropriate medical supervision. We will ask that you have this in place before supporting your project.

*Bisphenol A (urine): 0.414 ng/mL*

My daughter was throwing food on the floor. I turned her high chair to face the wall. This wasn't something I had done before and its perfunctory execution seemed strangely pedestrian. As she whined and complained, I was bothered by her segmented attempts to turn around, her raised hands swimming, soft-bodied. She was an overturned beetle, a turtle on its back. Her incapacity was disturbing to me. I was on a balcony with no railing above a plaza fuelled by the secretionary courage of executive force. A proscenium framed humid antechambers of questionable decisions in which cultivated attributes were bandaged and dressed for work. My greatest fear is to be helpless, vulnerable, incommensurately scaled to my torment. I gave her the plastic water bottle she loves. The one with the princess's exaggerated eyes.

## HORMONE

*

Commands spread
horizontally
in a crowd,
like a dream
surviving the difficulty
of imagining
how anyone survives
being asleep.
I don't recognize
myself
in the deadpans
of the deeds
I have done.
The bite marks
are blurry
and the wound
is swollen
with parts of me
that have given
their lives.
Pure as angels,
their heaven
is hot
to the touch.
My stomach
aches with indoor
exercise, adapting
itself to the walls
that compound it.
Interstitially, we wait
for you, O Lord.

A command
does not end
when it is fulfilled,
but remains stored
forever
in the children
surrendered
to the venial sense
of how right we are.
The fight against
flight
is the hypnagogic
origin of swelling.
The fluid is very clear
on this point.

*

*Streptococcus mutans*

Hunger is always gamed by quorum sensing. Enough cup holders eat drive-thrus. Enough drive-thrus eat long suburban commutes. Shift work eats the microflora that eat your lunch. Out west, the highways are grass-fed and the Alberta Advantage is one way of learning to feel a gingival recession. At the community centre, overfed bodies heave overboard into glittering tap water. Table sugar accumulates and must be cleared from the streets. Like commemorative plaques from our centenary cakes, once the pleasure centres are discovered, we leave the stove on for entire forests and stop brushing. Some foods make us even hungrier. It makes sense that the germs would want to kill and mount us.

## HORMONE

*

What do you call
that feeling
when your own

two fingers
are feeling
each other?

Sudden growth
makes a powerful
impression,

but its half-life is living
under an assumed name
beside the heat

from a gas station hot dog.
No matter how great
an idea begins to appear,

it is always torn apart
by the crowd
and fed to birds

who've known
no other life
than the owl-

decoyed ledgers
of this guttered city.
The simplest

form of power
is derived from a person's
own body

weight pressing downward.
Sit on your hands
and they'll feel you.

*

*Clostridium*

Activated charcoal and a raw egg. The cleanse was the longest she'd ever tried and it left her feeling weak and irritable. There was work to be done before the end of summer, so she hired a student from the list down at the Employment Office. He had his own car – a rust bucket, it turned out, but it was enough to get him out of the city and into the woods where she lived, tucked away on a rural road dotted with upscale homes and shot-up mailboxes.

She hired him because she wanted someone who wouldn't enter her house. He arrived in the morning, ate his lunch in the forest, and was gone again by the late afternoon. The stench of poorly combusted exhaust necklaced her driveway as he roared off. Everything happened outside. Instructions were issued through a crack in the door, her eyes peering out of the darkness like nostrils.

When it came to hygiene, she assumed the worst. Deep in the woods it was clear the clusters were fixing their nitrogen. In the absence of soap, the cleanse recommended washing with ashes. She sent him in with a wheelbarrow borrowed from neighbours to rake the forest down to its coals. No more deadfall littering itself. Each load was dumped in the ravine.

The metals and their magnets made her dizzy. They were seeding clouds now with barium, she'd read. She could taste the pesticides in her food – very faint and high pitched, but they were there like a mood afflicting salivary nipples with rainsticks. Saliva, she knew, was her blood filtered of cells. All day long, it went on pooling just behind her bottom front teeth.

She wanted him to dig a grave for her elderly dog. She had been a breeder, and quitting the business meant waiting out the fading livery of her celebrity stock. The pet cemetery was strewn in a far corner of the yard like a ripped-up coat of arms. He dug a plot while the last one living played around his legs. As summer wore on, the dog refused to die. Every morning, stiff but eager, it rose to meet him, observing the progress of his raking from blackened patches of earth. It sat there, a loaf of purebred head with crossed paws. Eventually, she threaded a bed sheet through the window for him to cover the plot. Weeds sprung from the mounded dirt.

It made her uncomfortable to think of her insides. Small things can be blown out of proportion. A cleanse was a house swept clean with a stool loosened by a body committed to water. Expulsions have always taken the form of rivers, or boats on rivers tipped over a height of land raised on masts of impoverished thought. Get the hell out. Wipe down the counters and walls. Roll up the carpets and beat them.

Her family fled Poland during the war. To check on his progress, she would stand on the sunburnt deck and tell him about her childhood in Mile End. She lived down the street from Mordecai Richler. 'Morty,' she said the kids called him, and watched slices of dark cake slide from the edge of her yard.

When it rained, he got wet. When it was hot, he got wet. Her house was a kidney. Whatever came in waited off-balance in the hallways and bedrooms stacked in taxonomical distress. Newspapers and milk jugs grew brittle in the chapped-lipped light of incurable stairwells. From the back yard, he could see her sunroom buckling with blistered garbage bags. 'Jesus, Mary, and Joseph,' the neighbour said to him after he asked to borrow the wheelbarrow, 'have you seen the inside?'

By the end of August, the cleanse had left her unsteady and she stumbled trying to change a light bulb in the front hall. He wrapped her arm using ice from his lunch cooler. She had let him in through the front door and from there he took in the intestinal diversity of intractable remainders, the sentimental detachments, the spore-forming units. He changed a few other bulbs by standing on a pile of phone books from formerly unmerged municipalities. She wanted to keep the burnt-out ones, but he carried them to his car.

Later that fall, she wrote him a letter. The dog was still alive and the light bulbs were working. Her arm could extend to its full length. She'd kept the ice he had given her. It was waiting in the freezer, having assumed the shape of its bag.

## HORMONE

*

The crowd reasons
like a fatty acid.
By eating

the heart
of a courageous foe,
bravery

may be acquired.
Because transparent
pieces of ice

melt in the mouth,
so too must panes
of glass.

*

## A BROMIDE

*Polybrominated diphenyl ether, # 47 (serum): 5.623188 ng/g lipid*

The umbrella is the starting point for a larger obfuscation. A constant mist of tiny particles rains upward, like neck hair at the cicada sex of a smoke alarm. Children outgrow the behaviours of cats, but for many years they are derelicts of skin flakes, stair runners, and upholstery. The average carpet smokes three packs a day. The glassy bits scratching your throat are leftover deterrents to predators. Dust is a conversation happening just out of earshot, it's the street talk of the Endocrine and Alderaan systems, a vector for the invectives of misdirection. Dust is a bunch of nickels your uncle gives you to get him another Goldschläger. My thoughts, like every other coagulation cascade, are made of melted lint and move around with the chirality of lost oven mitts. In the dusty barns of Michigan, the wrong bag of pale grit was mixed into cow feed. Nine million people ate Firemaster. My limbs tingle just out of broadcast range. Here come the industry standards to burn down the roofs of our mouths.

I developed blisters from walking, but I devised ways to deal with them, which included wax, tape, and music. I realized that when I walk, my right foot makes a slight twist at the end of my stride. Usually, after about eight to ten kilometres, depending on the monotony of the terrain, I could expect a blister to form on the outside of my little toe and then spread to each toe on my right foot. Soon, it would be general, all over the dark central plain of my foot, on the treeless hills.

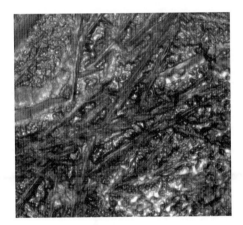

## PARTS PER BILLION

*Polybrominated diphenyl ether, # 100 (serum): 1.608696 ng/g lipid*
*Polybrominated diphenyl ether, # 154 (serum): 0.1063768 ng/g lipid*

We want revolution, but it's raining and Clayton has his sweatshirt on, the one with thumb holes burnt through the cuffs. Our high-schooled commitment is diluted by aerosolized anthems squelching from wet leaves and rotten stumps at the edge of his parents' farm. I can tell, by the point of his thumbs, he's not really into this. It barely burned when I lit it. More of a shrugged smoulder, more like watching your parents have sex – not explosive revolt, but the sudden, sodden commitment to an obvious and pedestrian crossing. I have what's left of the thing jammed down my boot when his mother appears. She's driving me home. 'You know that's really offensive,' she says. Her face stiffens in the maxed-out defog as we pass the conveyer belt factory at the edge of town. 'You shouldn't burn flags.' She's trying hard not to look at me and I feel the cauterized nylon edges against my sock, the thin plastic souvenir pole pressed to my ankle. She thinks there's something wrong with me but can't say it. We pass the car dealership with its checkered pennants and sodium lights. It's the year-end blow-out. The rain has ignited into snow.

## HORMONE

*

A body
is a crowd
getting out
of bed.
It feels
and enjoys
itself through
the genitals,
nose,
inner thigh,
belly button,
nipples, curled
toes, small
of the back,
lips, scalp,
ear lobe,
nape
of the neck,
and backs
of the knees
in a circular
motion,
with its
chemicals
it can never
be lonely.

■

## THE WOMEN FAVOURED THE SMELL OF SHIRTS
## FROM MEN WHOSE IMMUNE SYSTEMS WERE
## MOST DIFFERENT FROM THEIR OWN

*Actinomyces gerencseriae*
*Actinomyces graevenitzii*
*Corynebacterium durum*

I arrived at the gate panting. My connection from Philadelphia to Montreal hadn't left yet, so there I was, sweat trickling down the small of my back. Flight announcements crested over the fatigued lounge like drowned duck-rabbits. She appeared beside me, weaving slightly back and forth. 'Hi there.' Faint red wine stains continued a smile at the corners of her lips. Several cancelled flights had meant a five-hour delay and five more doubles at the bar. She asked why I was going to Montreal and I told her it was to read poetry. 'I like tall men.' She stared at me and I looked for something to look at just as the boarding announcements coughed to life. 'Fuck it! I am getting on that plane as soon as they open the goddamned door!' she said as she pushed ahead of the businessmen with their interlocking brick-work carry-on. I eventually found her sitting one row behind me. The seat beside me was empty and I could tell from her glance that she would claim it in a heartbeat once the aisle became free. A large, apple-shaped man finally sat down; his oversized presence made any seat adjustments, including my own, out of the question. I was trapped. She was sitting in the exit row beside a wary, willowy young Québécoise, whom she accosted with broken but unselfconscious French. The flight attendant came by to verify the fitness of the exit row passengers. I was certain they would move her. She was obviously drunk and would in the event of an emergency undoubtedly prove a catalyst for confusion. Despite several unsuccessful attempts at her attention, the bored flight attendant decided she was fit and moved on to some downstream arguments about the overhead bins. This was when the notes started to appear. Barely legible on a folded boarding pass pressed into the crook of my arm: 'Poet, I seriously need it. Will you join the mile-high club with me?' I had never been propositioned this way before. I thought about my body and the sweat still moistening my back. I thought about what it feels like to look at yourself from the outside, from, say, an airplane, peering down on farmland during shoulder season, headwaters visible all the way to their alluvial fans. 'I only understand kilometres,' I wrote back. She implored again and I declined with the excuse that the bathrooms were too small for a man like me. After the flight hit cruising altitude, she crept up behind me and whispered in my ear: 'You better be there in ten minutes. Don't be a pussy.' I felt heavy in my seat pressed against the oversized apple-body of my neighbour, who pretended to notice none of this. There she was waiting for me in the bathroom of a regional Bombardier Canadair jet somewhere over the Adirondack Mountains. After ten minutes. After twenty. She came back and pulled open the collar of my shirt. She threw a note against my chest. It said, in surprisingly clear handwriting with a small heart dotting the 'i': 'you make me sick.'

## HORMONE

✳

Us on that boat.

Us on that boat.

Money aside.

For the journey by boat.

The boat.

Was crowded.

Got on a boat.

And came here.

I was crying inside that boat.

We thought they were fishermen, but it was a boat.

My boat was a dinghy.

Nobody on the boat expected.

The water.

I took a boat to Italy.

They pushed us on the boat.

Our lives in that tiny boat.

On the boat.

By boat.

A boat.

I stop breathing.

Every time we think.

Of that boat.

✳

*Streptococcus pseudopneumoniae*

A few months ago, a small survivalist militia set up camp in my airways. They were friends of a family friend. No big deal. They seemed like a tight group and were fond of sharing feverish postulates about the Superdome and herd immunity. We ate together, drank together. But mostly they kept to themselves and their own routines in a harmless slick equipped with small watchtowers and channels to exchange nutrients. I didn't feel a thing. Then, sometime in February, I was getting run-down, pulled in too many directions. Standard mid-winter shit. This must have spooked them. I was up late one night with a slight chill, when abruptly they turned on me, fleeing the nasal passages, planting false flags in my bloodstream. They split up and tried different routes to safety, desperate to escape their doomed host. Some got stuck in my lungs and middle ear, taking momentary refuge under the forest cover of cilia. Their panic became a dispersed virulence that provoked inflammatory denunciations of the body parts they fled. White blood cells were forced to improvise my periphery. I coughed up more phlegm than any awakened interest in the experiences of others should reasonably permit. There I was, shot up on the inside by some patriots quitting their colonies for the quixotic promise of a cellular pastoral. During the migratory phase of self-interest, everything looks ballistic. I, for one, refuse to believe that someone at the very top didn't know about this.

The urge to defecate commonly occurs to people browsing in a bookstore. The *Mariko Aoki Phenomenon*, as it is called, afflicts me when I look at maps. The exquisite network of rivers in a drainage basin. 1:50,000 scale. I drew maps of my walks, their discharge.

## HORMONE

✳

It's really pathetic.
Fallacy
of the bearded climate.
Change is gonna come

to the car-washed
air masses.
Fire all bullets
directly into hurricanes.

Outcries tempo humidity,
cymbal stands
crash with the market.
Sequence is the great orderer

and destroyer.
Sequence
has made mountains
with campaigns

of sand and raised
the obscure cell
to the presidency.
It's the Baroque

staircase to bread
that fogs blood.
Insulin, like
the Wolffian and Müllerian

ducts, waits for signatures
on each colonnade.
Which part of me
was speaking

this rash?
Which part
was shouting directions
above the hapless haploids

confused
by the weather?
My greatest work of art
is heat.

*

*Chromium (blood): <2 nmol/L*

*Manganese (blood): 7.69 ug/L*

We cannot save snow. Snow can't be saved. No amount of intervention or therapy in the groups of anonymous Christian soldiers will work. Sacrifice won't keep it from dying in its place. Snowflake by snowflake, it can't be steered from ruin. If caught in an open palm and brought forth as evidence, it is done. If breathed on, it is done. There is no coming back after falling into rivers. Storms made of snow appear in the streets like insurrections lit by moths, or milkweed, or the cephalization of sympathetic distress. The possibility for transformation is real, the long awaited overthrow is here. And just like that it is gone. There is no other world. Wear a dark coat to see snow on your sleeve fugitively, phantasmagorically, before it goes. Even now it is stained red by the carotenoid pigment of a cryophilic algae. It falls orange on Korea with dust from the deserts of China. It has turned yellow in the Ural Mountains with high concentrations of manganese and chrome. It is black and greasy to the touch from smoke stacks of the Ohio and Rhine. Eat it by the handful and it enters you to be imprisoned in your cells, put to work in the ovens of your metabolism. Snow can't be saved. We cannot save snow.

## HORMONE

*

When I put food
in my mouth,
I am taking dictation.
I am reading
as I lick the glue
on the envelope
that holds the letter
I have written
about how you taste
to me. Small
nipples carpet
tongues and soft
palates, the cheek
and upper esophagus.
Receptors line
creases in the lungs
sensitive to the tripwire
taste of infection.
An enzyme
appears on sour-
sensing cells
for the exclusive
purpose
of deciphering
bubbles in a glass
of beer.
In Mexico,
as an act
of humble devotion,
a sect of Capuchin
nuns wore a groove

into the floor
by licking the length
of a courtyard
with their tongues.
There is a region
of the cortex
dedicated to the flavour
of water warmed
by the sun.

*

The sunburn occupies a complex cultural, biological, and medical position. Widespread social interest in tanning and the therapeutic effects of the sun have historically waxed and waned. Sun exposure is a major risk factor for skin cancer. However, it has also been associated with strengthened bones, reduced risk of heart disease, and reduced risk of other cancers. It has been used as a treatment for various autoimmune illnesses. In addition to being necessary for the production of vitamin D, sunlight also makes us feel good – it triggers the release of serotonin and endogenous opioids such as endorphins. Despite mutagenic effects, ultraviolet light is an important component of general health in ways that are still being understood. Sunlight is the only carcinogen we require to keep us alive.

The sunburn can be read as a message from the stars, our star, written into (at least temporarily) the kinked staircase of our genes. What does it say about the complicated matter of thresholds, about too much and not enough, about science and pseudoscience, about this world and the cosmos beyond? The capitalist Anthropocene has enabled industrial practices that have damaged the ozone layer and led to increased ultraviolet light penetration. These anthropogenic effects have augmented the sun's message. Similarly, the proliferation of sunscreens has posed other potential problems. There is evidence that the parabens commonly used as preservatives in sunscreens are hormone-mimicking endocrine disrupting chemicals. Parabens have been found to be associated with some melanomas. What if sunburns were trying to tell us something? Who might they be a message from?

*Ethyl Paraben (urine): 1.66 ng/mL*

I am radiantly happy. The people around me squint in the blaze. I feel this way even as cutaneous pigments empurple small bonfires around which carnivorous communiqués edit my bearings. The line between tonic and poison is the line between tonic and gin. Cancer is always a risk of reading too deeply. Through my head the sun wanders with its surrogate ashtrays, suddenly ermine among bloom-freighted cocktails eyelashing the dermal contiguity of vaulted esteem. In times of pleasure we must decide again and again how to undress our blisters. A room is always brightest under its shades.

# VITAMIN D

*1,25-dihydroxycholecalciferol*

addleheaded
condiddled
dadded

daddled
deadheaded
dendrodendritic

diddered
diddled
disbudded

disgodded
disindividualized
dodded

doddered
dogsledded
dunderheaded

granddaddy
lepidodendroid
muddleheadedly

skedaddled
underbudded
woodshedded

## MEAT SWEATS

*Corynebacterium*

It was cloudy, but I burned anyway. A binary message dripped down my back. Like a city that is otherwise a victim of its rivers, my sweat smells the way it does because of the creatures that live in it. Out of the heat, my shirt dries white with salt. I have about three shakers full inside me right now. On the skin where the burn glistens, there is a microbe shaped like a club that sends its own messages to the outside world from within a reflective pool of perspiration. Found in pig saliva and in the fruiting bodies of truffles, this chemical signal can influence how much someone likes my haircut, smile, or the unconscious habit I have of slightly revealing the tip of my tongue. With warm shoulders still full of obscured daylight, the beacons continue well into the night, microbes alive at the pool-side switch. I am a city whose roads are merely widened trails cut by creatures looking for salt.

*Isopropyl Paraben (urine): 0.748 ng/mL*

By the time it appears, it has already happened. Dali's lobster is a boiled telephone. Napoleon goes to St. Helena. The sun never sets on the British Empire so the whole thing burns to a crisp. At some point, aspiration owes its origins to recumbency, just as pigments don't always come from ink but also shadows lying on the page. Warmth and dizziness are red flags raised on a moon whose real portents are footprints. Affection for refrigerants is incremental. Opioids pool among the lesser lengths of a psychic centre peeled the way an apple is fully grasped by being eaten. The lights stay on all night and no one sleeps. The stairs are swept. Thymine to Thymine. Uracil to Uracil. The sun doesn't oblige us to do anything, only something. All the stems await their cells.

## HORMONE

We can take this park!
By the gut flora!

We can take this park tonight!
Our shit is the compressed sum of all the evidence against us!

We can also take this park another night!
It stinks and cries to heaven!

Not everyone may be ready tonight!
We get rid of it alone in separate rooms!

Each person has to make their own autonomous decision!
It is clear we are ashamed of it!

No one can decide for you. You have to decide for yourself!
Our real glory derives from our grip!

Everyone is an autonomous individual!
Everyone is an autonomous individual!

*

*Streptococcus*

Next to the off-leash area after dark, a man struggles to release a dog from his car. A few snowflakes avoid themselves while falling. He is at the open door fevering his weight. There is fur spilling over the steering wheel, jumping at his mouth, but there is no dog. A woman's head rises and falls, her hair mixing with the man's hand. Her bra visible against her bare back. He moves in and out of her and the snow moves in and out of the car goosebumping her shoulder blades. They move together, changing planes in the endorphin airports that concourse through their bodies, that guided them to the edge of this park in the first place and left the map-reading light lit to bathe them in the sepia mesh of historical arrival.

Looking inside my body has done something to my body. This park and its No Dumping signs are reproduced in cities that reproduce on the edges of larger cities like galvanic corrosion. It is not possible to separate the form of desire from its material substrate. The engines rev and the redistributed world burns. It makes perfect sense to fuck here. I appear suddenly walking my dog as pointlessly corrected grammar in the bootlegged snow, a dirty sentence diagrammed by the dial tone of the keys still in the ignition. Our eyes lock as I pass. Beyond the parking lot, I pick up after my dog. Through the thin plastic bag I hold her shit and feel the temperature of the inside of her body.

My pee comes out with such contrasting heat that it fogs my thinking. I am an individual for the purposes of involuntary valves. What gives a company the right to its teeming instructions? I am letterheaded. I tried to have the animal mounted in a pose that I remembered it being in before I decided to end its life. In the throes of digestion, the small intestine spreads out to cover twice the area of Central Park, or the length of ten thousand footsteps. We envelop what we eat. Like bacteria. Like flame retardants. Like a people who, after some time together, are shared by the same desires. Here is my body and everything in it. Let the aliens take me to their mothership piece by piece.

**HORMONE**

You've been
a difficult crowd.
But you've been
my crowd.

And when you
leave, my
blood cooling
like a ruled-out

thought,
the elaborate
fiction
of my immune system

convincing
no one,
broken camps
leaching

nitrogen
and potassium,
fungicides
and uranium

from my last
dressed shadow,
you won't look back.
The nucleus

of terms
has split.
All messages
are homeless

before they're received.
Even the ones
we leave
for ourselves.

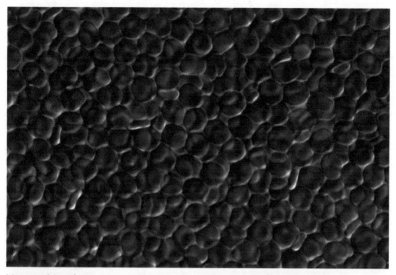

You can love the questions, but you do not have to love the answers.

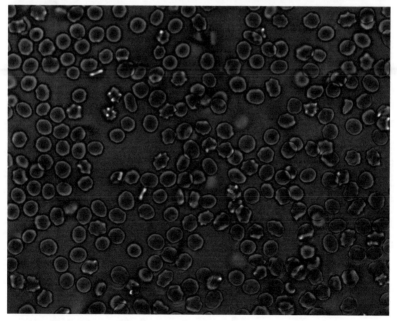

Information cascade (with platelets).

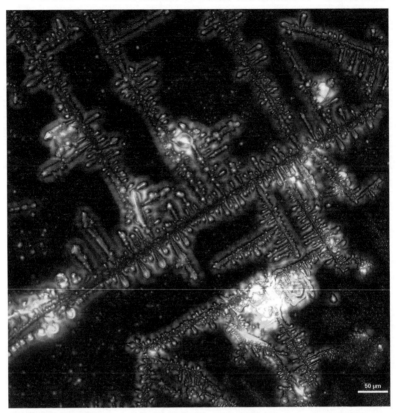

50 μm

The faster I walk, the less of me there is. I'm worried I sweat more than I used to.

An unrooted phylogenetic tree depicting the relationship between bacterial species found in my gut.

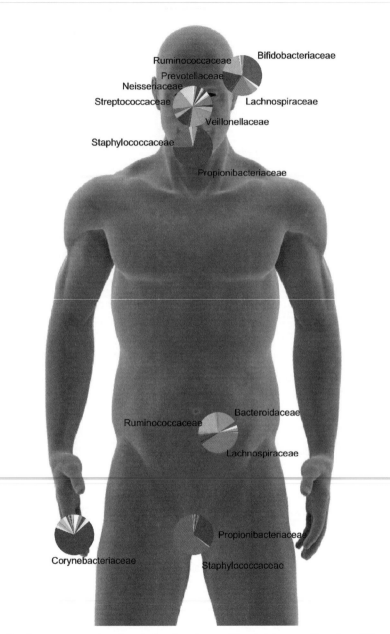

Pie charts representing the relative abundance of bacterial genera found on different parts of my body.

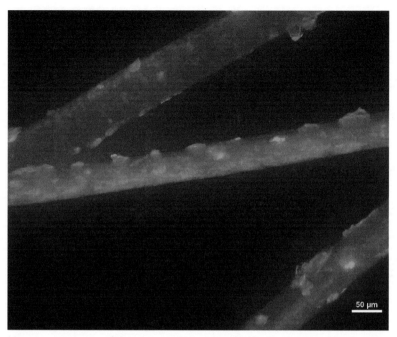

Hair is an extension of the nervous system. Is it feeling the inside or the outside?

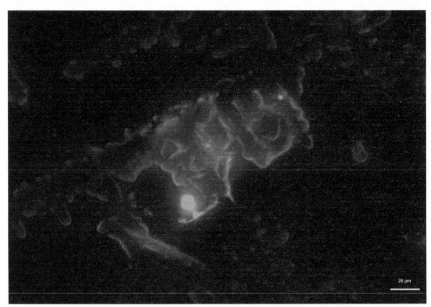

My crystallized sweat in full sun.

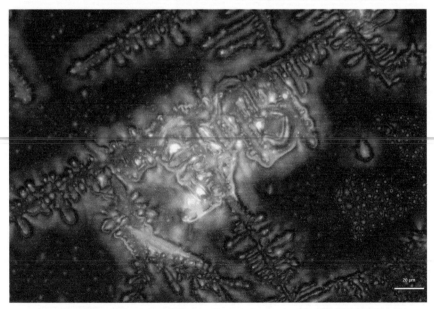

I don't have the same body that I used to have. I don't have a body in the way that I understood a body.

fr... ...a collar of pearls and glass ... ...d put
it ar...nd his n...k. After hav...g proceeded ...ong th...reet,
...e of...e serva...s ...ame br...g...g ...o ...for...of
...sh fish, enclose...in...roll...hich we...e m...de ...n
the shells...colored...w...riv.nkles,...'...th
in high es...ati...an...om each co...d...er...ed...
golde...p...w...s, fni...in...very p...e...anner, abo
foot...a h...in length. ...h...e...ere broug
Moctezuma turn...d, oward...them round m
neck: ...ut then r...al...the st...t in the order
already...nti...ached a...ry large and
splendid...in w...we we...e to be quartered, ...ich
...fully prepare...for...r re...ption.

He then to...k...by t...nd and led me int...spacious
salon, in...ont...ch w...a court, thr...v...ich we
entered. Having c...ised me to sit d...wn o...piece of rich
car...ting, which...e had ordered to be made fo...own
use...he told...wait...is return...re, and then
away. After a short space of time, when...people were all
best...ed...the...arter...returned...th many and
va...ou...jewels of...d and silver...feather wor...and five or
six ho...pieces of...ton clo...ery rich and of varied
te...re and finish.

A quotation from Cortes's second letter to Charles V describing his meeting with Moctezuma in Mexico on November 8th, 1519. It is colonized with bacteria that I swabbed from money and swabbed from my hands after touching money. The crowd of microbes, the result of the interaction between bodies and systems of exploitation and exchange, has been invited to participate in the creation of an erasure text.

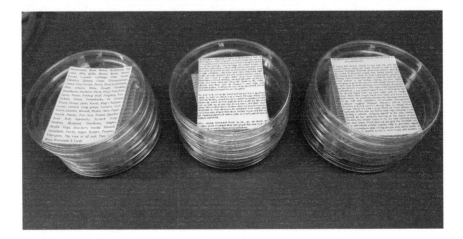

Can writing function as a productive hormone disruptor within larger cultural narrative sequences? This is my urine. Its metabolites are messages.

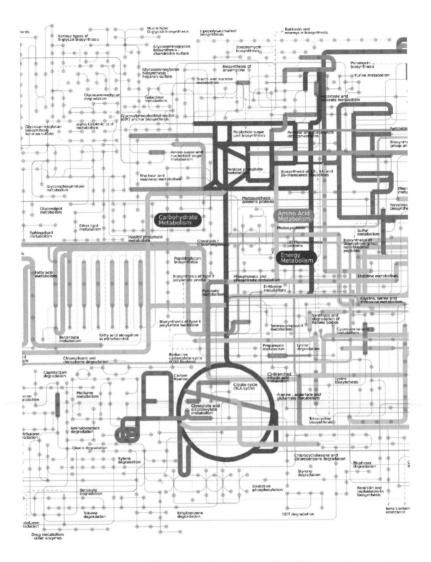

A diagram showing how different functional genes found in my gut connect to each other to form metabolic pathways. The most frequent trips on the underground. The most obvious conclusions.

What does it look like to take the hormone as a method for writing?

The individual is a capital letter. Can we use it to spell something else?

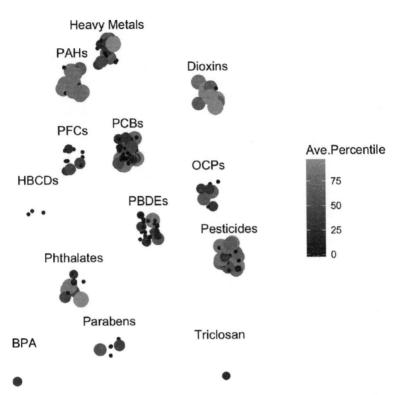

The relative concentrations of chemicals in my body compared to human males my age in Canada and the USA. Chemicals in similar classes are grouped together.

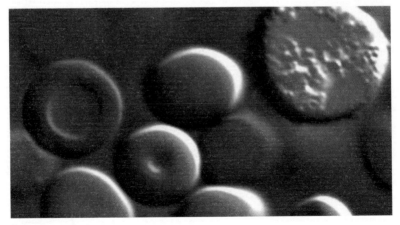

Surveillance footage.

Bamboolah, Bank, Beans, Benjamins, Big
Ba ones, Bills, Boffo, Bones, Booty, Bread,
or Bucks, C-notes, Cabbage, Cake, Cents,
Cheddar, Cheese, Chips, Chumpchange,
Clams, Coin, Cream, Dancy, Dead presidents,
Dibs, Dinero, Dime, Dough, Doubles,
Doubloons, Ducketts, Flesh, Float, Fins, Five-
spots, Fivers, Folding stuff, Frogskin, Fun-
tickets, Green, Greenbacks, Gs, Grand,
Gravy, Honey, Jacks, Keesh, King's Ransom,
Large, Lettuce, Long green, Loonies, Loot,
Lucre, Lumber, Moolah, Nickel, Ones, Paper,
Payola, Plaster, Pop cans, Pound, Quarter,
Quid, Roll, Sawbucks, Scratch, Scrip,
Shekels, Sharpnel, Simoleons, Singles,
Skrilla, Slugs, Smackers, Smoke, Smoosh,
Spondulix, Stacks, Sugar, Tender, Tenners,
Ten-spots, The root of all evil, Two bits,
Wad, Wampum, X, Yards

Money harbours significant quantities of microbes and chemicals. Other words
for money.

Ba... ...an, ...an. Beans, Benjamins, Big
ones, Bills, ...offo, Bones, Booty, Bread,
Bucks, ......, Cabbage, Cake, Cents,
Che.. ... Chee....irs, Chumpchange,
Clams, Coin, C...am, Dancy, Dead presid...'s,
Dibs, Dinero, Dime, Dough, Dc bles,
Doubloons, ...ts. Flesh ...oat, ins, Five-
spots, Fivers, Folding ...uff, Frog... Fun-
tickets, Green, ...reenbacks, Gs, Gr...d,
Gravy, Hon..., Jack, Ke...n, King's ...som,
Large, Lettuce, Lor... gre...n, ...o...s, ...,
Lucre, Lumber, ...olah, ...kel, ...n..., Paper,
Payola, Pla...er, Pop ...ns, ...d, Quarte...
Quid, Roll, Sa...uch..., Scratch, Sc...p,
Shekels, Sh...nel, Simoleons, Singles,
Skrilla, Sl..gs, S...acke..., S...c...e ...noos...,
Spond...ix, ...cks, Sug...r, Ten...er, T...ers,
Ten-spots, The ...ot of ...l evil, Two bits,
Wad, Wamp... ...Y...s

Other words for money edited and revised by bacteria cultured from swabs of money.
Phthalates are present but not visible.

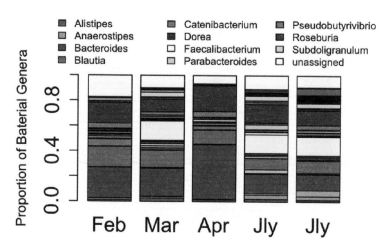

At the genus level, how does my composition change over time?

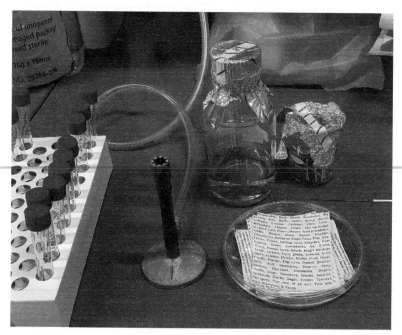

At work on my composition.

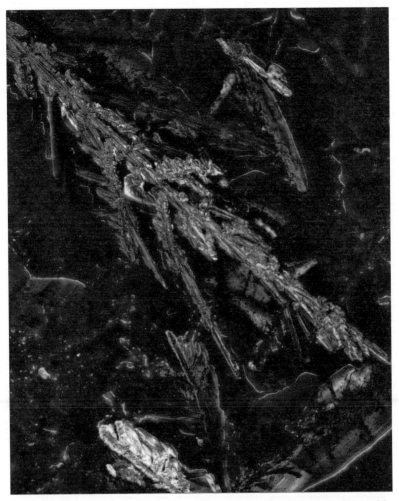

Being able to read the chemicals and microbes in bodily fluids means being able to read the writing of the Anthropocene in ways we have not been able to do yet, in ways that might illuminate the common crowds we bear and the crowds in common that we are.

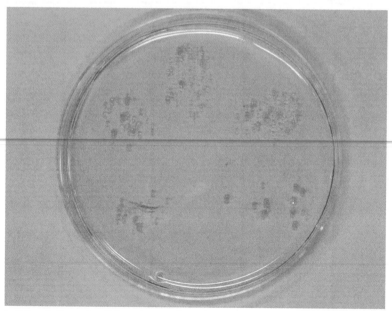

Right hand, fingertips.

Left hand, fingertips. What else touches what I touch?

This book uses the hormone as a compositional method, with its emphasis on concentration, cascade, and sequence. A long poem in sections, called 'Hormone,' runs throughout, with the chemical and microbial poems floating in amongst these streaming segments. In its various manifestations, 'Hormone' includes appropriated and altered texts about crowds. The main sources include Gustave Le Bon, *The Crowd: A Study of the Popular Mind* (1896), Elias Canetti, *Crowds and Power* (1962), and Jodi Dean, *Crowds and Power* (2016).

The list of microbes at the beginning of this book represents a comprehensive catalogue of all the microbes I discovered in and on my body at the family level. While all the epigraphs to poems in the book that refer to bacteria identify organisms discovered during my tests, the names may not always appear in the same form on the list at the front. This is because in the epigraphs I have occasionally referred to these organisms at the species, genus, order, or higher taxonomic levels. The list of chemicals also at the front of the book refers to all of the substances I was tested for. I have at least trace amounts of many of these chemicals.

'Agents Orange, Yellow, and Red' (p. 15) was written in response to the chemical 2,3,7,8-Tetrachlorodibenzodioxin, which is also known as dioxin. Dioxin is a pervasive environmental contaminant. It has been used to manufacture paper, and also herbicides like Agent Orange. It was also used, rather clumsily, in the attempted assassination of Viktor Yushchenko in 2004.

'Mouthfeel' (p. 25) responds to microbial changes caused by the Western diet. High sugar and high fat have resulted in gut microbiomes commonly dominated by the phyla *Firmicutes* and *Bacteroidetes*. This poem concerns sugar specifically. While its precise effect on the Western diet remains unclear, there is research that suggests the ratio of *Firmicutes* to *Bacteroidetes* is influenced by sugar intake. In particular, the abundance of *Catenibacterium mitsuokai* and *Bacteroides* appear to be affected.

The sixth section of 'Lipids' (p. 39) responds to the unusual sex ratio of girls to boys born in Aamjiwnaang First Nation, near Sarnia, Ontario. The community is surrounded by approximately 40 percent of Canada's chemical industry. While PCBS have been implicated in altered offspring sex ratios, and while the poem implicitly associates the circumstances in

Aamjiwnaang with PCBS, I want to emphasize that the matter is complex and as yet unsettled. Many other factors and chemicals may be involved. For more information on the people of Aamjiwnaang and citizen science initiatives (including 'bucket brigades') associated with the community's activism for environmental justice, see Sarah Marie Wiebe's *Everyday Exposure: Indigenous Mobilization and Environmental Justice in Canada's Chemical Valley*. Vancouver and Toronto: University of British Columbia Press, 2016.

The image of the enzyme *beta-fructofuranosidase* from *Bifidobacterium longum* (on p. 42) is from the Protein Data Bank. PDB ID: 3PIG. Bujacz, A., Jedrzejczak-Krzepkowska, M., Bielecki, S., Redzynia, I. and Bujacz, G. (2011). *FEBS Journal*, 278: 1728–1744. doi:10.1111/j.1742-4658.2011. 08098.x.

'Shotgun, Called It' (p. 43) begins with an epigraph that illustrates the amino acid sequence for the enzyme *beta-fructofuranosidase* from *Bifidobacterium longum*.

'Commensalism' (pp. 45–48) emerged in part from the discovery that I have a family of bacteria on my skin called *Methylophilaceae*. As it happens, these organisms are abundant in the mouths of dogs and are often transferred to people who live with dogs. The term 'commensalism' describes a neutral relationship between two organisms that results in no harm being done to either participant, despite the fact that one may benefit from the relationship. The early domestication of dogs would have followed a commensal pathway. Commensal microbes play important roles in the human gut.

'OCD' (p. 52) and 'Independent Variables' (p. 124) concern *Enterococcus and Streptococcus* bacteria, which, along with several other species, are important in stimulating the production of serotonin. Due to interactions between bacteria and human cells, 90 percent of the body's supply of serotonin is produced in the gut. Associated with feelings of well-being and necessary for the maintenance of human moods more generally, serotonin is a neurotransmitter whose production in the human body is largely outsourced to nonhumans. Research has suggested a link between Obsessive Compulsive Disorder (OCD) and insufficient levels of serotonin in the brain.

The title of the poem 'The People of Grassy Don't Have a Mercury Problem, They Have a Drinking Problem' (p. 65) is a paraphrase of a pervasive and persistent prejudice expressed during the 1970s by, among others, the largely white community of Kenora toward the Indigenous residents of nearby Grassy Narrows. The community of Grassy Narrows had been and continues to be poisoned by mercury spilled into the Wabigoon-English River system in the 1960s by a pulp and paper mill in Dryden, Ontario. I found mercury in my blood and it made me think about my connection to this issue of racial injustice as a privileged settler in southern Ontario.

'Gut-Brain Axis' (p. 74): Microbes in the gut can influence the brain. Increased abundance of the genus *Alistipes*, for example, has been connected to depression and anxiety. *Escherichia coli* and *Bacillus* species are associated with the production of neurotransmitters such as serotonin, norepinephrine, and dopamine, which can influence mood and personality.

'Disruptors' (pp. 77–88): While endocrine disruption and its effects on normative notions of masculinity occur as recurrent points of focus in this book, and in this poem in particular, it is my intention to critique and satirize a culture of masculinity for which endocrine disruptors pose a particular kind of anxiety. I am interested in the nature of this anxiety, but I am also interested in exploring the broader, eco(hetero)normative issues associated with endocrine disruptors.

The section of 'Hormone' on page 91 appropriates and alters text from 'A transcript of Donald Trump's meeting with the *Washington Post* editorial board' from *The Washington Post*, March 21, 2016.

'Scale' (p. 94) concerns Bisphenol A (BPA), which is a chemical used, among other applications, in thermal paper for receipts, in linings to food and beverage cans, and to make clear, durable plastic baby bottles. It is an estrogen-mimicking hormone-like substance.

'Heterotrophies' (p. 97): Typically colonizing the human mouth, *Streptococcus mutans* are major contributors to tooth decay and other oral diseases.

'The Cleanse,' (pp. 100–102) concerns bacteria in the genus *Clostridium*. Found in soil and in animals, including the intestinal tracts of humans, *Clostridum* are opportunistic spore-forming species capable of both benign and pathogenic behaviour, depending on the circumstances within a host. Some forms of the bacteria can also initiate metabolic activities in humans that affect mental health.

'A Bromide' (p. 104) and 'Parts Per Billion' (p. 106) include chemical epigraphs that reference Polybrominated diphenyl ethers, which belong to a class of compounds known as brominated flame retardants. PBDEs leach from common consumer products like TVs and carpets. Household dust is believed to be the greatest source of contamination for humans.

The section of 'Hormone' on page 110 appropriates text from interviews recounting the terrifying experiences endured by migrants crossing the Mediterranean Sea to Europe. "I'd rather die at sea than stay there': migrants on crossing the Med' from *The Guardian*, May 16, 2015.

'Interkingdom Signalling' (p. 111) borrows textually and conceptually from Deborah Franklin's article 'What Makes Good Bacteria Go Bad? It's Not Them, It's You,' published August 8, 2013, in NPR's online Public Health section.

The section of 'Hormone' on page 116 responds to Jason de Haan's art work entitled 'Capuchin Tongues' and is an altered excerpted version of work commissioned by the Esker Foundation in Calgary (see below).

'Spectrum,' 'The Sun Can Kill You,' 'Vitamin D,' 'Meat Sweats,' and 'I Hope You Are Feeling Better' (pp. 118–122) are part of a larger work originally commissioned by the Esker Foundation in Calgary in response to an art exhibition by Jason de Haan (*Oh for eyes! At night we dream of eyes!*) and Anton Vidokle (*The Communist Revolution was Caused by the Sun*) in 2017.

'Vitamin D' (p. 120) is a list of words in English in which the letter 'D' occurs in every word four times. Not to be confused with Vitamin D4 (22-dihydroergocalciferol), found in certain mushrooms, this vitamer is the linguistic form of this fat-soluble secosteroid.

'I Hope You Are Feeling Better' (p. 122) appropriates and alters some of the language in the introduction to Alexander Chizhevsky's (Tchijevsky) 1926 paper 'Physical Factors of the Historical Process,' translated by Vladimir P. de Smitt.

The images of the phylogenetic tree and my metabolic pathways (pages 131 and 137) were created with the assistance of the following sources: Yamada T et al. (2011) Nucleic Acids Res doi: 10.1093/nar/gkr313; Letunic and Bork (2016) Nucleic Acids Res doi: 10.1093/nar/gkw290.

## ACKNOWLEDGMENTS

I gratefully acknowledge financial assistance provided by the following organizations: the Canada Council for the Arts, the Ontario Arts Council, the Social Sciences and Humanities Research Council of Canada, and the Humanities Research Institute at Brock University.

Thanks to the Banff Centre for a residency in the Leighton Artists Studio and to the Banff International Research Station's Creative Writing in Mathematics and Science Workshop.

Chemical testing was done at l'Institut national de santé publique du Québec (INSPQ) and at SGS AXYS Analytical Services Ltd. I acknowledge the assistance of the Silent Spring Institute in Newton, MA, USA, for providing necessary interpretations of biomonitoring data. Microbiome sequencing and analysis were conducted by uBiome and American Gut. Microscope images of my blood cells, urine, sweat, and hair were produced with the assistance of Jeff Stuart in his laboratory at Brock University.

I thank the following people for research assistance, technical guidance, laboratory work, and imaging: Gail Ackermann, Laura Birkett, Monica Drenth, Jordan Froese, Jose Gabrie, Amanda Graveline, Heather Gordon, Embriette Hyde, Jimmy Limit, Will Ludington, Lucas Maddalena, Daniel McDonald, Phil Miletic, Ruthann Rudel, Ana Sanchez, Cassandra Scavetta, James Sidney, Evangelia Litsa Tsiani, Alison Waller, and Sarah Wiebe. Thanks also to my colleagues in the English Department.

Some of these poems appeared in earlier versions in the following publications: *Big Energy Poets: Ecopoetry Thinks Climate Change, Boston Review, Canadian Literature, ESC: English Studies in Canada, Environmental Humanities, Evening Will Come* (The Volta), *Fueling Culture: 101 Words for Energy and Environment, Joyland Magazine, NewPoetry, The Goose, Vallum,* and in the chapbooks *The Betatext* (Chromium Dioxide Press), *HIJ Reading Series No. 8* (Book*hug), and *Sleeper Cells* (The Olive Reading Series). Thanks to all the editors involved.

A section of this book was a finalist for the 2016 Canadian Broadcasting Corporation (CBC) Poetry Prize. Another section was commissioned by the Esker Foundation in Calgary as part of a 2017 art exhibition. Versions of poems from the book have also been written using and exhibited with the 3D Poetry Editor, developed and curated by Michiel Koelink, Jon Ståle Ritland, and David Jonas.

Thanks to St. Michael's Hospital in Toronto for coming to my aid when I was bleeding and terrified.

Thanks to everyone at Coach House Books and in the writing community who has encouraged and inspired me.

I thank my family and, above all, my wife, Erin Knight. I could never have survived this book without her.

**Adam Dickinson**'s poetry has appeared in literary journals and anthologies in Canada and internationally. He is the author of three previous books, including *The Polymers* and *Kingdom, Phylum*. His work has been nominated for the Governor General's Award for Poetry, the Trillium Book Award for Poetry, and the ReLit Award. He was also a finalist for the CBC Poetry Prize and the K. M. Hunter Artist Award in Literature. He teaches poetics and creative writing at Brock University in St. Catharines, Ontario, Canada.

Typeset in Aragon and Aragon Sans.

Printed at the Coach House on bpNichol Lane in Toronto, Ontario, on Zephyr Antique Laid paper, which was manufactured, acid-free, in Saint-Jérôme, Quebec, from second-growth forests. This book was printed with vegetable-based ink on a 1973 Heidelberg KORD offset litho press. Its pages were folded on a Baumfolder, gathered by hand, bound on a Sulby Auto-Minabinda and trimmed on a Polar single-knife cutter.

Designed by Alana Wilcox
Cover design by Ingrid Paulson
Cover art is from Giltsch, Adolf, Lithographer, and Ernst Haeckel. *Ascomycetes*. Schlauchpilze., 1904. [Leipzig und Wien: Verlag des Bibliographischen Instituts] Photograph. Retrieved from the Library of Congress, https://www.loc.gov/item/2015648954/. (Accessed February 12, 2018.)
Author photo by James Sidney

Coach House Books
80 bpNichol Lane
Toronto ON M5S 3J4
Canada

416 979 2217
800 367 6360

mail@chbooks.com
www.chbooks.com